Praise for *The Four Purposes of Life*

"Dan's new book offers concise and practical guidance for living a meaningful life with a clear sense of purpose."
— Deepak Chopra, author of *The Soul of Leadership*

"This book skillfully delivers on its promise of bringing renewed meaning and purpose — for anyone seeking clear directions at one of life's crossroads."
— Ken Dychtwald, founder of Age Wave and author of *A New Purpose*

"Dan Millman reminds us of the power of our essential humanity, how to touch it and use it to make this a better world."
— Thom Hartmann, author of *The Last Hours of Ancient Sunlight*

"During one of the darkest periods of my life, Dan's writing in *Way of the Peaceful Warrior* extended a hand to me and helped pull me into the light. Dan is the personification of 'love, laugh, live, and give,' as you will see in his new book, *The Four Purposes of Life*. In this book, he does it again as only he can."
— Quincy Jones

"Leave it to Dan Millman to come up with a way of making purposeful decisions and helping us see deeply into the center of each moment…a graceful and wise book."
— Elizabeth Lesser, cofounder of Omega Institute and author of *Broken Open*

"Important reading."

— Edgar Mitchell, *Apollo 14* astronaut and author of
The Way of the Explorer

"Dan Millman, a great teacher, shares important rules to help people everywhere improve their lives, find their passion, do what they love, and live with inspiration."

— Don Miguel Ruiz, author of *The Four Agreements*

"A refreshingly practical yet profound approach to living your sacred calling."

— Peter Russell, author of *From Science to God*

"Dan Millman's new book distills pearls of wisdom with simplicity and power. It's a wake-up call to live our best life. His personal stories highlight stages we all encounter. Reminding us of our own purpose, Dan shows how to integrate all our knowledge in the present moment. It's a book we can revisit many times."

— Amy Smart, actress and environmentalist

"A wonderful book with extremely helpful practices for finding one's authentic purpose. Highly recommended!"

— Ken Wilber, author of *The Integral Vision*

"Once again, Dan Millman provides us with keys to a well-lived life. This is a lovely read, filled with meaningful insight."

— Marianne Williamson, author of *A Return to Love*

THE FOUR
PURPOSES
OF LIFE

Books by Dan Millman

The Peaceful Warrior Saga

Way of the Peaceful Warrior
Sacred Journey of the Peaceful Warrior
The Journeys of Socrates
Peaceful Warrior: The Graphic Novel

Guidebooks

The Four Purposes of Life
Wisdom of the Peaceful Warrior
Everyday Enlightenment
The Life You Were Born to Live
No Ordinary Moments
The Laws of Spirit
Body Mind Mastery
Living on Purpose

Inspiration

Bridge Between Worlds (with Doug Childers)

Children's Books

Secret of the Peaceful Warrior
Quest for the Crystal Castle

For further information:
www.peacefulwarrior.com

THE FOUR PURPOSES OF LIFE

**FINDING MEANING AND DIRECTION
IN A CHANGING WORLD**

DAN MILLMAN

H J Kramer

published in a joint venture with

New World Library
Novato, California

An H J Kramer Book

published in a joint venture with

New World Library

Editorial office:
H J Kramer Inc.
PO Box 1082
Tiburon, California 94920

Administrative office:
New World Library
14 Pamaron Way
Novato, California 94949

Text design by Tona Pearce Myers

Library of Congress Cataloging-in-Publication Data
Millman, Dan.
 The four purposes of life : finding meaning and direction in a changing world
/ Dan Millman.
    p.   cm.
Includes bibliographical references.
ISBN 978-1-932073-49-2 (hardcover : alk. paper)
1. Life. 2. Vocation. 3. Meaning (Philosophy) I. Title.
BD431.M623 2011
128—dc22   2011001245

First printing, April 2011
ISBN 978-1-932073-49-2

Printed in Canada on 100% postconsumer-waste recycled paper

g New World Library is a proud member of the Green Press Initiative.

10 9 8 7 6 5 4 3 2 1

To my parents,
Herman and Vivian Millman,
who gave me the freedom
to find my own way.

The purpose of life is a life of purpose.

—— ROBERT BYRNE

CONTENTS

Prologue: *Living on Purpose*   1

THE FIRST PURPOSE:
LEARNING LIFE'S LESSONS

• *Smarten Up* • *Grow Up* • *Wake Up*   9
   Voluntary Adversity   16
   The School Rules   17
   Humanity's Curriculum   18
   Required Courses   19

THE SECOND PURPOSE:
FINDING YOUR CAREER AND CALLING

• *Choose Satisfying Work* • *Earn a Good Living*
• *Provide a Useful Service*   31
   The Essence of Career and Calling   34
   Stories of Career and Calling   36
   Self-Knowledge and Career Decisions   48
   Talents, Interests, and Values   52
   Career Criteria: The Trinity of Needs   61
   Career Decisions: Analysis and Imagination   67
   Time Travel with Your Subconscious Mind   71
   Deciding to Decide   74
   Career Notes: From Entry Level to Leadership   75
   How Will You Spend Your Life?   81

THE THIRD PURPOSE:
DISCOVERING YOUR LIFE PATH

• *Understand Your Hidden Calling*
• *Follow Your Higher Potential*   89
   Hidden Calling, Higher Potential   92
   Determining Your Birth Number   96
   Your Birth Number and the Third Purpose   97
   The Nine Life Paths   98
   Putting It Together   106
   Individual Differences, Shared Patterns   109

Fundamentals on Your Life Path 110

Life Paths, Career Paths 112

Insight Isn't Enough 115

Keeping the Faith: Your Promise and Potential 117

THE FOURTH PURPOSE:

ATTENDING TO THIS ARISING MOMENT

• *Pay Close Attention* • *Make Each Moment Count* 119

The Man Who Had No Purpose 122

What Snood Taught Me about Life 124

Life as a Series of Moments 126

There's No Such Thing as a Future Decision 127

We Cannot Grasp the Now 129

The Challenge of Attending to the Present 130

The Gift of Life: A Matter of Perspective 132

The Highest Practice of All 134

Epilogue: *Our Spiritual Purpose* 139

Acknowledgments 145

Further Resources: *Source Material* 147

Appendix: *Determining Your Life-Path Number*
  by Doing the Math 151

About the Author 153

Prologue

LIVING ON PURPOSE

*I think the purpose of life is, above all,
to matter; to count, to stand for something,
to have made some difference
that you lived at all.*

— LEO ROSTEN

WITH THE PACE OF LIFE ACCELERATING, in a world of change, it's not easy to maintain our balance and sense of direction. Yet we strive to do so, because a sense of direction, toward a meaningful goal, may be the better part of happiness. In this pursuit, the journey may indeed matter more than the destination — but without a destination to aim for there is no journey; we can only wander.

We humans are goal seekers from infancy, drawn by the objects of our desire. But somewhere along the way, most often in the dilemmas and angst of adolescence, a sense of confusion obscures the simple desires of childhood. What we *want* is muddied by expectations about what we (or others) think we *should* do. We begin to doubt our desires, mistrust our motives, and wonder where we're going and why.

In my first book, *Way of the Peaceful Warrior*, the old service station mechanic I called Socrates suggested that all seeking — for knowledge or achievement, for power or pleasure, for love or wealth or even spiritual experience — is driven by the promise of happiness. But the search only reinforces the sense of dilemma that sent us seeking in the first place. So he advised me to replace the search for future happiness with the *practice* of "unreasonable happiness" in each arising moment.

When my seeking ended and the practice began, I came to understand that what we all need, even more than a happy feeling, is a clear *purpose* — a meaningful goal or mission that connects us with other human beings. As Viktor Frankl wrote in his book *Man's Search for Meaning*, this fundamental need for purpose and direction may be as important to our psychological growth as eating is to our biological survival.

But the duties of our daily lives leave little time to contemplate life's larger questions, except on rare occasions, in the silent hours or in times of transition or trauma when larger questions arise: *What do I really want? How would I know if I had it? What would happen if I got it? Is getting what I want going to take me to where I want to be?* And finally, *What is the purpose of my life?*

Maybe you've wondered why you're here on Earth or what you're here to do — what the French call your *raison d'être*, your *reason for being*, an organizing principle and sense of direction that gives shape and meaning to your life. History provides numerous examples of iconic figures like Joan of Arc, Mohandas Gandhi, Nelson Mandela, and the Dalai Lama, whose clarity of purpose drew others to their missions like moths to the light.

This book, which contains elements from my previous works, presenting them in their full context for the first time, was inspired by my own quest for a purpose in life. I once believed that my purpose was all about work, and I searched through my twenties and well into my thirties for a career and calling. It took another decade of exploration and introspection before I understood that career is only one of four primary purposes in life.

But why *four* purposes? Some might argue that our sole (or soul) purpose is learning to love — that whatever the question, love is the answer — or that spiritual awakening or surrender to God is our ultimate aim. Others point out that our primary biological purpose is family — bonding with a mate, and bearing and caring for children. Still others might propose three or five or more purposes, or even suggest that there are as many purposes as there are people. Yet just as we divide all the days of the year into four seasons, and points on a compass into four primary directions, sorting our life experience into four fundamental purposes helps us to create a sense of structure within the totality of our life experience. These four purposes also prepare us for, and point toward, the ultimate or transcendental awakening promised by all the great spiritual traditions.

The first of four purposes we'll explore in this book — *learning life's lessons* — centers around the premise that Earth is a school and daily life is our classroom, and that our daily challenges (in the core arenas of relationship, work and finances, and health) bring learning, growth, and perspective. The value of our life experience resides in what we learn in the process. Difficult days may provide the most important lessons, helping us develop the awareness and self-reflection that lead to higher wisdom.

The second purpose — *finding your career and calling* — underscores the critical importance of self-knowledge, as well as integrating both logic and intuition, in making the wisest possible life decisions. This section also shows how the service you provide in the world can become a meaningful path of personal and spiritual growth.

The third purpose — *discovering your life path* — addresses a hidden calling you're here to explore, a personal path that for most people remains obscure. The information in this section sheds light on the strengths you possess and challenges you face, bringing clarity to a deeper mission you're here to fulfill.

The fourth purpose — *attending to this arising moment* — brings the first three purposes into sharp focus and down to earth, enabling you to integrate all the others with awareness and grace, within the fold of each arising moment.

I wrote this book for anyone seeking deeper insight into themselves and their lives, but especially for those at a crossroads, facing a challenge or change, when "business as usual" no longer applies. Join me now as we explore the four key purposes that provide meaning and direction in a changing world.

The First Purpose

LEARNING LIFE'S LESSONS

• Smarten Up • Grow Up • Wake Up

The wise learn from adversity;
the foolish repeat it.

— PROVERB

EARTH IS A PERFECT SCHOOL, and daily life is the classroom. This idea is hardly new, but what follows will help you appreciate the full value of your life experience. And once this central premise penetrates your psyche, you'll stop seeking and start trusting — because you'll confront a higher truth: You aren't here on Earth merely to strive for success; you're here to *learn* — and daily life is *guaranteed* to teach you all you need in order to grow, and evolve, and awaken to your higher purpose here.

You are evolving even now — and there is no way to fail as long as you continue to learn. Like a stone slowly polished by the river's flow, we're shaped over time by the currents of life. The Indian saint Ramakrishna once observed, "If you try to open a walnut when the shell is still green, it is nearly impossible. But when the walnut is ripe, it opens with just a tap." The classroom of daily life serves your ripening process.

SOME YEARS AGO I RECEIVED A LETTER expressing a dilemma shared by many: "Since reading your first book I've had a growing interest in spiritual practice, but how can I find the time when I have a wife and three children and a full-time job?" I wrote back to remind the writer that his wife and children and work were his most important spiritual practices — because true practice is not separate from daily life but rather its very substance. As writer Adair Lara put it, "And some, like me, are just beginning to guess the powerful religion of ordinary life, a spirituality of freshly mopped floors and stacked dishes, and clothing blowing on the line."

Daily life, and the journey it represents, will remain your master teacher. This book serves as a map to help orient you along the way and guide you through the school of this world.

Here are some reminders about how the process of learning works in the classroom of daily life:

Lessons repeat themselves until we learn them. Sometimes we hear a wake-up call but prefer to pull the covers over our heads so we can slumber and dream a little longer. We may ignore, resist, rationalize, or deny reality for a considerable time. That's okay — our schooling is entirely self-paced, but the lessons keep coming until our actions change.

If we don't learn the easier lessons, they get harder. Resistance to learning (or change) reaps more dramatic consequences over time — not to punish us but to get our attention. As Anaïs Nin wrote, "There came a time when the risk to remain tight in a bud was more painful than the risk it took to blossom."

We learn and grow through challenges, and every adversity has hidden gifts. We've all experienced physical, mental, and emotional pain. Yet each challenge has brought a greater measure of strength, wisdom, and perspective. We may not welcome a challenge or embrace unexpected change, loss, or disappointment, but looking back, and over time, we come to appreciate the gifts of adversity.

Oh, please! you may think. *I've heard all this before*: "When God closes a door, God opens a window." "Every cloud has a silver lining." "What doesn't kill us makes us stronger." But I will not spout platitudes or preach "positivity." The fact is, pain and difficulty are no fun — I speak from my own experience.

Some years ago, when a motorcycle crash left me with a shattered thighbone, my recovery was difficult; it also changed the course of my life. I started asking bigger questions and opened to new paths that might have otherwise remained beneath my notice. And climbing out of that deep hole gave me the strength to scale inner mountains. I certainly don't recommend bone fractures as a method of personal growth, yet I've learned to view every difficulty as a form of spiritual weight lifting — and we're all in training.

My injury was one of millions of difficulties that people suffer every day on planet Earth, from debilitating illness to childhood abuse to soul-wrenching poverty. Yet the potential for growth remains. In the November 26, 2010, "Letters" section of the *New York Times Magazine*, Betty Rollin wrote:

> 35 years after my first mastectomy and 26 years after the second, I'm feeling oddly cheerful about the whole cancer experience — not that I'd recommend it. But I slowly came to realize that just because something is awful doesn't mean you can't benefit from it. Awful things happen to a lot of us, and it's a happy moment when you start noticing some kind of payoff. Cancer survivors, for example, notice that they're breathing, the way other people don't. And because they're breathing, they're grateful in a way a lot of people aren't, and grateful is a good place to wind up in life. It beats Poor Me.

We all slip into the "poor me" mode at times — like the person who once asked me, "Why does life have to be so difficult?" I answered, "You want life to be easy? Then don't get married or have children; don't take on any responsibilities or form any attachments; always do the minimum, never volunteer; live small. Your life will then seem easier. But are we humans here on Earth to live the easiest possible life? Or are we here to grow stronger and wiser?" I believe that St. Augustine knew the answer, which is why he said, "Lord, I ask not for a lighter load, but for stronger shoulders."

Of course we can find easier and more efficient ways to accomplish our goals — no need to seek out adversity or create unnecessary complications. But meanwhile, life will continue to serve up a varied menu of challenges that contribute to our growth and evolution. Events will arise that are neither predictable nor controllable; we can't alter the waves that roll in, but we can learn to ride them. As my old mentor Socrates once observed with a shrug, "Sometimes you get the elevator, and sometimes you get the shaft." Yet, as cancer survivor Betty Rollin and countless others understand, unexpected benefits can emerge out of great adversity, which is why we sometimes volunteer for it.

Voluntary Adversity

Choosing to train in sports or music, preparing for college or graduate school exams, acting, painting, and practicing other arts are all forms of voluntary adversity, as we must confront inner and outer obstacles along the way, facing self-doubt and frustration. The demands of training reveal our weaknesses and develop our strengths. So commitment to any endeavor can become a path of personal growth.

Daily life provides other forms of voluntary adversity as well. For example, maintaining a long-term relationship and raising children, for all their pleasures and joys, present significant challenges; so do responsibilities in the business world and caring for elderly parents. There's something for everyone in the school of daily life.

Many forms of adversity are *involuntary*: a drunk driver slams into us, we lose our job or a loved one, or we get a cancer diagnosis despite healthy eating and exercise. But we do volunteer for many, if not most, of our daily challenges — we sign up and step willingly into the fray. For example, you have chosen (or made choices leading up to) whom you're with right now, where you live, and what you're currently doing. By taking full responsibility for your past choices, you reclaim the power to make new ones. And as you make the best of your life, your life will also make the best of you.

As Socrates reminded me in *Way of the Peaceful Warrior*, "The way itself creates the warrior. We are all peaceful warriors in training, and every life is a hero's journey."

The School Rules

In addition to our core curriculum (which I'll soon present), our Earth school has a clear set of rules, also known as natural or universal laws. These school rules reflect reality — the mechanics of our universe. They also provide guidance about how to function wisely and well in the course of our schooling. So the better we understand and respect these laws, the smoother goes our education.

In science, universal laws are described with mathematical precision, as in the equation $E = mc^2$. In religion, these laws take the form of, for example, the Ten Commandments, the teachings of the Talmud or Koran, or the Golden Rule.

These laws, or school rules, are based not on moral concepts but rather on action and consequence. While some claim that morality comes from above, others suggest that morality is a human invention. Moral precepts differ from one culture or era to another, which is why philosopher Bertrand Russell proposed that "sin is geographical." But the wise among us have observed that actions lead to consequences and lessons. Whether we learn these lessons — or whether they have to repeat themselves — depends on our current readiness and openness.

The natural world reveals and reflects universal laws in their purest form. Observe, for example, how trees need strong roots but flexible branches if they are to withstand powerful winds; how streams flow gracefully around obstacles, finding the path of least resistance; and how the seasons change in their natural order.

The school rules, revealed in the course of daily life, provide a reality-based approach to living that I call the *peaceful warrior's way.* By observing and aligning our lives and actions to these laws of reality, we learn, grow, and evolve with amazing grace.

Humanity's Curriculum

If Earth is a school, what courses do we need to pass in order to graduate? Some years ago, the answer came to me in the form of twelve core subjects — a specific curriculum hidden within (or behind) the activities of everyday life. These subjects are include self-worth, discipline, well-being, money, mind, intuition, emotions, courage, self-knowledge, sexuality, love, and service, which I outline below in the catalog of "Required Courses."

In this perfectly designed, fully integrated curriculum, all subjects are equally significant, and all are required. We may be tested in the area of health or money one day and encounter a pop quiz in courage the next. There are no grades, only pass or fail. A pass indicates progress; a fail provides an opportunity to learn and do better the next time. (So there is no permanent failure, only the need to repeat the course and continue with that line of study.) Bear in mind that spiritual life begins on the ground, not up in the air — even Olympians start with the basics. As your skills improve in each of these areas, you'll begin to experience the true meaning of success in the form of higher states of clarity, energy, and action.

Required Courses

As you read the following summary descriptions of the twelve core subjects in life's curriculum, reflect on your current progress in each, as well as on what improvements are still possible on the path to self-mastery.

Foundations of Self-Worth: Getting Out of Your Own Way

Life provides certain opportunities and choices, yet we allow ourselves to receive, achieve, or enjoy such opportunities only to the extent that we believe ourselves deserving or worthy of them. A well-known parable advises, "Ask and you shall receive." The question is, what are you willing to ask for and strive for? As Ramakrishna put it, "An ocean of bliss may rain down from the heavens, but if you hold up only a thimble, that is all you receive." So if we operate on the belief that "beggars can't be choosers," then few options appear. Low self-worth is a primary cause of self-sabotage. Few of us consciously sabotage our relationships or finances, but we may wonder at times, "Why did I say that? Why did I do that?" This first course in the school of life helps us to shift from holding up only a thimble and saying, "Oh, I really couldn't accept that" to opening our arms and saying, "Yes! Thank you!" Realizing your innate worth expands your horizons and opens you to a larger life.

Roots of Will: The Practice of Self-Discipline

Most of us know the value of regular exercise, good diet, kindness, relaxation, and breaking unhealthy habits. Our greatest single challenge in every area of self-improvement is transforming knowledge into action — turning what we know into what we actually do. While some of us act without thinking, too many of us think without acting. Willpower isn't a mysterious force that descends on us from above; rather, it is an innate power within each of us, waiting to be applied. We do so every time we accomplish a task (like taking out the trash or doing the laundry, office work, or schoolwork) despite a lack of motivation. So this subject, which you face daily, calls you to reclaim your will by following through with your goals. As your skills and understanding improve, you better appreciate that your life will be shaped largely by what you do each day — whether or not you feel like doing it.

Well-Being: Approaches to Health and Vitality

Your body forms the foundation of your earthly existence and is the only possession you are guaranteed to keep for a lifetime. Its care and feeding are key to all else. An energized body enhances strength, mental acuity, healing, social interactions, and every other human capacity. While genetics plays a powerful role in health and longevity, you have wiggle room — it's called *lifestyle* or daily choices. The previous two foundation courses in the school of life — self-worth and self-discipline — open the way to an energizing, healthful lifestyle. This course, over time and through your own experience, teaches the wisdom of regular, moderate exercise, a balanced diet, and sufficient rest — amplifying energy for all other courses in the school of life.

Money and Values: Establishing Stability and Sufficiency

Earning, spending, and saving money preoccupy many of us, who spend a good portion of each day working for more of it. But for those of us who have a religious or spiritual interest, money remains suspect — a topic of mixed feelings best expressed by the late boxing champion Joe Louis, who said, "I don't really like money, but it calms my nerves." We eventually learn that money is a form of energy that only makes us more of who we already are — it can bind us or free us, depending on how we manage it. This course cannot guide everyone to great wealth but rather shows the way to create sufficiency and stability, sometimes even leading to the deep satisfaction of philanthropy. As the Arabic proverb goes, "If you have much, give of your wealth; if you have little, give of your heart."

Exploring the Mind: The Nature of Your Inner World

This subject in the core curriculum helps us to understand the illusory nature of our subjective mind. Lao-tzu advised, "As soon as you have a thought, laugh at it," because reality is not what we think. We perceive the world through a window colored by beliefs, interpretations, and associations. We see things not as *they* are but as *we* are. The same brain that enables us to contemplate philosophy, solve math equations, and create poetry also generates a stream of static known as discursive thoughts, which seem to arise at random, bubbling up into our awareness. Such mental noise is a natural phenomenon, no more of a problem than the dreams that appear in the sleep state. Therefore, our schooling aims not to struggle with random thoughts but to transcend them in the present moment, where no thoughts exist, only awareness. Our mind's liberation awaits not in some imagined future but here and now.

Introduction to Intuition: Accessing Subconscious Guidance

Whispering beneath our everyday awareness is a child-like consciousness — a shaman, a mystic, a weaver of dreams and keeper of instincts. Our subconscious mind (or body-wisdom) holds keys to a treasure-house of intuitive guidance and survival skills. It helps us to make fully informed decisions, and may save lives in times of danger. Daily life eventually teaches us the value of trusting intuitive messages and, in the words of Zen sword master Taisen Deshimaru, learning "to think with the whole body." Nearly all scientific discoveries come from creative flashes of intuitive insight (later tested and verified using the scientific method). For this reason Einstein proposed that imagination is more important than knowledge. As we learn to let intuition become reason's trusted adviser, we integrate reason and faith, building a bridge to wisdom and a new way of sensing our world.

The Nature of Feelings: Achieving Emotional Freedom

Emotions play a central role in human life. Behind all seeking is the desire to feel *good* (happy, content, fulfilled, confident) *more of the time* — and to *feel bad* (anxious, sad, angry, fearful) *less of the time*. In the United States and abroad, people spend billions of dollars on self-medication and buy countless books offering to replace bad feelings or thoughts with good ones. Meanwhile, emotions continue to rise and fall like waves on the sea, of their own accord, passing like clouds in the sky. But over time, the school of reality teaches us to accept, value, and learn from our emotions without trying to fix or control them — and without letting them determine our behavior. Life reveals that we have more control over our behavior than we do over transient emotions or thoughts. This realization helps us liberate our lives from reactive or confused soap operas and establish stable, mature, and responsible behavior. We learn to ride the shifting tides of emotion like skillful surfers as we grasp the great truth that we don't need to *feel* compassionate, peaceful, confident, courageous, happy, or kind — we only need to *behave* that way.

Fundamentals of Courage: Confronting Our Fear

In this subject area we confront the primal emotion of fear, which can lead to paralysis or power, and can end a life or save it. Fear can warn us of genuine danger; it can move us to prepare well, take precautions, or avoid a situation. It can also burden our lives with anxiety or self-doubt. How many of us avoid opportunities due to fear of the unknown? We may also fear rejection, failure, and even success. In the classroom of daily life, we learn to listen to fear's counsel when our physical bodies are at risk. But when we experience a more subjective fear of embarrassment, looking foolish, or feeling rejected, we feel the fear but act with courage. Courage is not the absence of fear but the conquering of it. Heroes feel the same fear as cowards; they just respond differently.

Knowing Yourself: Finding Wholeness in the Shadows

In childhood, our power and charm come from authenticity — our actions are undiluted by subterfuge or hidden agendas. But as the years pass, we learn to tell social lies and use pretense to please or placate others while disowning the disapproved-of parts of our psyche. In this way, we create a shadow persona constructed from fragments of our full identity and potential. But as we mature and begin to grasp that we are often the cause of our own difficulties, we begin a process of compassionate self-observation leading to deeper self-knowledge — denial gives way to authenticity as the light of awareness penetrates our shadow. We come to accept ourselves (and others) as we are rather than as we might want ourselves (or them) to be. And as we embrace the full scope of our humanity, we open the way to genuine growth and transformation.

Your Sexual Life: Understanding the Pleasure Principle

Our drive for sexual intimacy is as natural as thunder-showers or the changing seasons. But if we suppress or exploit our sexual energy, we create obsessions, compulsions, and guilty secrets. This course of study in the realm of relationship shows us how to observe, accept, enjoy, and channel sexual-creative energy rather than merely indulging or denying it. Whether we are young or old, sexually active or not, an abuse survivor or "perfectly adjusted" — and no matter what our sexual orientation — we all have areas to explore. Sexual issues are rarely about the sexual act. More often than not, our complications stem from unrealistic beliefs, fear, insecurity or jealousy, and issues of identity. Our course-work in life includes, but also goes beyond, our physical drives into areas of awareness, balance, trust, openness, honesty, and the courage to achieve true intimacy.

The Mastery of Love: Awakening the Heart

Despite the efforts of poets and philosophers through the ages, love defies definition. It may appear as sentimental infatuation or as a chemically induced hormonal state, sexual pleasure, familial devotion, or anything that makes us feel good. We know that the word *love* can be either a noun or a verb, and that love is something we can feel and also something we can do. Our life experience reveals the evolving nature of love as it changes from an emotion that happens to us, rising and falling out of our control, to an art we can learn — from something we receive to something we give. As we mature, this practice of love liberates us from dependence on the changing tides of emotion. We gain the capacity to show loving-kindness to others even when we don't feel like it. This is the power of love and the heart's education.

Service and Meaning: Completing the Circle of Life

We all know that service is a good thing — that serving others lifts us out of exclusive preoccupation with the self and turns our attention out into the world. But service is not only something we do for others; it is also an act of self-transcendence — anything we do without regard to self-interest. This final course in our schooling provides an essential link that fulfills all the others. Service is a form of yoga, a catalyst of friendship, an affirmation of our common humanity. Even the smallest gesture of self-sacrifice — giving of our time, energy, or attention — shifts our focus from "What's in it for me?" to "What is for the highest good of all concerned?" Every service we provide for others represents the fruition of our spiritual maturity, completing both our curriculum and the circle of life. In service we find the master key to a meaningful, purposeful life that connects us to one another, and to our world.

BEFORE YOU MOVE ON TO THE SECOND PURPOSE, take a few moments to appreciate what you've already accomplished in each of the twelve subject areas in Earth's core curriculum — self-worth, discipline, well-being, money, mind, intuition, emotions, courage, self-knowledge, sexuality, love, and service — all the tests you've taken and lessons you've learned. But don't get so wrapped up in the twelve subjects we've covered that you lose sight of the larger purpose — *learning life's lessons* — which leads to greater wisdom, perspective, and appreciation for the value and significance of your daily life.

The Second Purpose

FINDING YOUR CAREER AND CALLING

• Choose Satisfying Work
• Earn a Good Living • Provide a Useful Service

Whatever your life work is, do it well.
Do it so well that no one else could do it better.
If it falls on your lot to be a street sweeper,
sweep streets like Michelangelo painted pictures,
like Shakespeare wrote poetry,
like Beethoven composed music;
sweep streets so well that
all the hosts of heaven and earth
will have to pause and say,
"Here lived a great street sweeper."

— MARTIN LUTHER KING JR.

EVERY PERSON ON EARTH — whether living in a well-heeled suburb, inner city, or rural village — possesses twenty-four hours each day, about sixteen of those hours in more or less of a waking state. Depending on available options, most people look for a productive way to spend those hours. And unless they are independently wealthy, most people in the developed world spend many of their waking hours in an office, at home, or outdoors doing work that provides a sense of purpose (and even pride) while performing a service to others. Some types of work primarily offer material rewards; other pursuits may bring in little income but provide psychological or emotional rewards.

Whatever your current situation — in school, seeking suitable employment, contemplating your next steps, making a change, or approaching retirement years —

the second purpose invites you to consider the work you do (or might like to do) in light of your interests, skills, and values; to take stock of your relationship to career and calling.

The Essence of Career and Calling

Because most people pondering their "purpose in life" are thinking about either their career or their calling, let's clarify the meaning of these two terms.

Your *career* refers to a service you perform — trading your time, effort, attention, knowledge, skills, and experience for a salary or other income and benefits. You may refer to it as your employment, work, livelihood, occupation, living, trade, vocation, profession, or "just a job." You may have many reasons to go to work each day — but unless you are independently wealthy, earning an income is a primary career motive.

Your *calling* refers to a personal interest, attraction, inclination, drive, or passion that is usually (but not always) of a higher order. It isn't just something you want to do, but rather something you *need* to do, something that captures your imagination, touches you deeply and absorbs you, whether or not you can explain why. A calling may (or may not) earn an income or become a career.

A calling can take the form of an art, craft, or other creative endeavor, such as writing, painting, or playing a musical instrument. Or it may involve volunteer service, such as teaching, working with children or the elderly, or charitable work. Some people, wanting to make a difference in their community or the larger world, are called to a religious order, others to military service, politics, or environmental (or other) causes. Parenthood — minding the home front and raising children — may be one of the highest and most fundamental of callings.

Since a true calling is often associated with serving others, personal leisure activities such as golf or bowling, hunting or fishing, sewing or reading, knitting or building miniature ships fall into the realm of hobbies or avocations. But if we end up performing or teaching that hobby, sharing it with others, then our avocation may become both calling and career — an absorbing professional path of learning and growth.

One child's interest in magic tricks may fade with the arrival of young love or some other passion; another child may end up a professional stage magician. One teen's love of video games may wane with age; another young person may become a gifted game designer. Similarly, many people have an interest in yoga, martial arts, or another fitness practice — but for some pioneers and popular teachers, their exercise immersion evolved into a lifetime calling and career.

The primary difference between a career and a calling is that we pursue a career primarily for income and a calling primarily for innate satisfaction. But if you love your career so much that you'd do it for free (if you could afford to do so), then it has likely become a calling as well. And if a calling begins to produce a good income, then it has also become a career.

Why are such distinctions important? Because many of us cling to a calling yet struggle financially because we ignore or resist the practical need for an income-producing day job, insisting, "I must be free to follow my heart and devote my life to my art." Others among us focus so much on climbing a career ladder to success that we abandon a life-affirming calling that might bring even more joy and meaning to our life.

For some of us, career and calling have merged into one; for others, they remain separate and distinct. One way is not necessarily better than another. We each have our own unique process.

Stories of Career and Calling

The following stories highlight different approaches to career and calling. Although I've changed the names and a few identifying details in the interest of privacy, these are true stories about real people — a tiny sample to highlight the variety of experiences people meet on the winding path to their career and calling.

I met Megan Caldwell at Oberlin College, where I coached the men's and women's springboard diving team. I'd rarely encountered a student-athlete who so loved her sport, or had more fun at it, than Megan, who was dedicated to perfecting her diving skills. (I was only vaguely aware that she was majoring in mathematics and physics.) That first year she won the Women's Conference Championships on the three-meter board.

After that, I moved on to another phase of my life and we were out of touch for two decades. During that time, Megan's life moved from reverse dives to inverse problems of acoustics and electronics. She earned a PhD from Indiana and did postdoctoral work at Stanford, eventually working on advanced radar technology, in which she transformed numbers representing voltages to coherent radar images for national defense.

Megan had established a strong career — but for nearly twenty years, except for occasional practice sessions, her athletic calling faded to fond memories. Then, in 1997, when she was in her early forties and doing research at the University of Minnesota, she found a course in beginning springboard diving and signed up. The instructor, seeing her skills and form, suggested that she compete in Masters Diving in her age group. She did so, and won several national titles and a Masters World Championship on the three-meter board.

Even as Professor Megan Caldwell was dedicated to her career, she remained devoted to her calling — springboard diving. Over a hot meal on a cold autumn evening in Berkeley, California, where she was a visiting professor at a math institute, I learned that she made time — three days every week — for a two-hour commute each way, by bus and train and on foot, from Berkeley to Stanford to practice with other Masters divers — on sunny days and in pouring rain (thank goodness for the hot-tub respites between dives!). She was then in the 55–59 age group, but her form, and love of her calling, remained that of the young woman I had first met all those years before.

Megan's life was blessed, but those blessings came from years of work and application. Her hard-earned career and calling were worlds apart, yet each has brought a special kind of satisfaction.

The following story makes quite a different point as it relates how a late bloomer found his calling and transformed it into a career with a surprising twist.

Kevin Kohler found his calling early on but showed little tolerance for paycheck-driven work. Kevin's passion during high school and college was the game of Ultimate Frisbee. His many hours throwing the flying disk led to a certain expertise, but his pastime showed little promise as a profession.

Eventually, Kevin's parents suggested that he move out of his childhood bedroom and into his own apartment — after all, he was by this time thirty-two years old. Soon after, while he was taking a hot shower, an idea popped into Kevin's mind. Thrilled by his revelation, he quickly dried off, dressed, and made a call to the Wham-O Corporation, which manufactured the Frisbee, and finally got through to a decision maker in their marketing department. "Here's my idea," said Kevin. "I'd like you to give me five hundred free Frisbees with the words *World Peace* written in both English and the Russian Cyrillic alphabet. Then I'd like you to pay my way to Russia and put me up for a month. What I'll do for you is to become a Frisbee goodwill ambassador — I'll go to Red Square every day, once we get permission, and I'll teach people to throw Frisbees. It will be a great cultural exchange and help open up a market for you."

This was back in the 1960s, during the Cold War. The company agreed, since it was not a big investment and might do some good. Kevin traveled to Russia (then part of the USSR), learned to speak the language, and ended up leading numerous Frisbee goodwill tours there. He even married a Russian woman.

Since Kevin couldn't find work that suited him, he did what he loved and got someone to pay him for it. His calling, for some years, became his career.

Not many of us will materialize a career (and calling) based on an idea that appears in a flash, but Kevin's life testifies to what's possible.

The story of Stuart Anders represents yet another approach to career and calling.

I met Stuart Anders for the first time when I began my four-year tenure as head gymnastics coach at Stanford University. With enthusiasm and zeal, I prepared to do whatever it would take to transform what at that time was a weak team into top-caliber athletes. I was twenty-two years old and, like many athletes my age, thought I was bulletproof. The year before, I had co-captained the UC Berkeley gymnastics team to their first National Collegiate Championships, so my standards and expectations were high.

Before my first day meeting the team, the athletic director drew me aside and explained, "Dan, for the past ten years, a man named Stuart Anders has been showing up regularly as a volunteer assistant coach. I realize that you don't know him, but he's a good guy and totally reliable. He only did a little gymnastics years ago, but he loves the sport. It's your call, of course, but it would be a nice gesture if you'd let him come in and help in any way he can." I said I'd be glad to meet with Stuart and see how it went.

As it turned out, he was a relaxed, easygoing guy with a likable personality, who did show up on time, every day. We didn't have much time to talk personally, since we were both focused on training. But it seemed that we'd get on fine.

Then one day a month or two later, Stuart arrived about an hour late. He apologized, explaining that he'd been out flying and a complication had kept him from arriving on time. Curious, and a little surprised that Stuart had a pilot's license, I asked, "What kind of plane were you flying — a Cessna or Piper Cub?"

"It's a larger craft," Stuart answered. "Boeing's newest, called a 747. I was checking its glide path." It turned out that Stuart was an aeronautical engineer and test pilot for NASA who worked at Moffett Federal Airfield in nearby Mountain View. I also learned that he restored old Porsches as a hobby and was building a one-man experimental jet, rivet by rivet, in his garage.

I quickly lost my twenty-two-year-old sense of self-importance, thinking about how my volunteer assistant had apologized for being a little late to practice. I had known Stuart only through one of his callings — helping young gymnasts hone their craft — even as he devoted most of his day to another calling and professional career, testing aircraft on the cutting edge of flight technology.

Now we turn to someone who chose a different path, following her heart's wisdom and a call to service.

Julia Marsala is an intelligent and industrious woman who loves to read and stay well informed. In high school she maintained close to a straight-A average, but in college, like many students in liberal arts, she lacked a clear career objective or path and changed majors several times. Despite her lack of career direction or ambition, Julia demonstrated a strong work ethic and an inclination for service, which would become a lifelong calling. As a child she helped out every day after school in a small market; in high school and college she worked at a variety of jobs out of the practical necessity of earning money. The type of work was less important than the idea of being useful. This service orientation is where Julia derived satisfaction, making her labors, however humble, feel worthwhile and meaningful.

After graduating from college Julia volunteered to teach at a school while earning money as a waitress. As the years passed, she remained indifferent to the idea of finding a profession. In fact, she never had to do a career search because work always seemed to find her. When Julia married, she worked as a bookkeeper and helped support her husband as he searched for his own career and calling.

With the birth of her first child, Julia's calling shifted naturally into the role of mother. For a time she consciously chose a life as a homemaker, while her husband focused on producing income. He was the breadwinner; she was the bread baker, providing a stable emotional foundation for her family. She embodied the saying "There's no such thing as a nonworking mother." Julia's life was not defined by or confined to the walls of her home. When her children started school, she worked part-time until her husband's income grew. And throughout her children's school years prior to college, she volunteered at school functions. Her life was not only full; it was a full-time job.

Over the years, Julia developed an interest, and then

some expertise, in mythology. She took numerous courses, read many books on the subject, and did her own research. She ended up speaking to a few small groups on mythology. But her studies remained a calling, not a career — one facet in a wide variety of roles, as she continued her higher calling of service to her husband, her children, and the world around her.

Not everyone chooses to have children, but those who do so may take a break in career pursuits to raise children as their primary service. Some may later return to a career outside the home; others find a lifelong calling as parents. Still others, like Julia Marsala, live full and meaningful lives without having to define themselves by a career, serving in whatever circumstances life presents.

The following narrative describes the multiple — and passionate — careers and callings of one of the most intriguing people I've known.

I was a college professor teaching various forms of physical training when Charles Edwards enrolled in my trampoline course. He struck me as an unlikely candidate for any gymnastics practice, since he was built more like a football tackle or grizzly bear. He was, in fact, a football and a field hockey player and a member of the college aikido club who worked part-time as a motorcycle mechanic. It turned out that Charles was also a bright young man. Near the end of his senior year, he applied to a number of medical schools.

Charles and I lost touch for nearly a decade. Then I learned that he had become not only a doctor but a top pediatric heart surgeon, performing some of the early transplants. He married Marie, also a physician and researcher, and eventually they had three children. Charles had achieved a third-degree black belt in aikido and was at the top of his profession when he decided to move from the fast track of the big city to a smaller practice in a rustic location.

Life went smoothly for Charles and his family for some years. Then, as he was working in his garage with a circular saw to make a birdhouse for one of his sons, he stepped on a spot of oil. His leg slipped out from under him and he fell. When Charles sat up, he discovered that two fingers from his right (dominant) hand were missing. As he recovered from the acute injury, he practiced intensely using his left hand to tie sutures and use instruments, but it became apparent that he would never perform major surgery again.

After some soul-searching, Charles decided to start law school. Perhaps it isn't surprising that he edited his school's law review and graduated with honors. Specializing in medical law, for years he served in hospital administration.

Charles had become a respected physician, attorney, and hospital policy maker as well as a high-ranking aikido sensei. As he and his wife watch their grown children move into their own careers and callings, Charles is now considering a new career and calling — divinity school. He exemplifies not only a life well lived in the service of others but also a life reinvented in response to changing circumstances.

I once asked Charles, "Where do you find the time to accomplish all that you do?" His reply might be a reminder to us all: "I never *found* the time, so I made some." Charles's life shows what is possible when a passionate engagement with life combines with a focused application of energy. His every endeavor has become his calling.

Despite the saying that "life begins at forty," we can sometimes experience a rebirth decades later. Retirees who have completed their career arc may find a new calling. Take the case of Bud Gardner.

Bud Gardner, former college English teacher, writer, and writing coach, prepared to follow his heart and play golf into his retirement years. Then he read a study about how playing a musical instrument late in life was good for aging brains (and spirits). So he surprised himself by buying a harmonica.

It wasn't entirely out of the blue; he had played old favorites on the mouth organ for sixty years, ever since his dad had taught him. Soon bored playing the same old three songs, he placed an ad in a local paper hoping to find someone to teach him more. After twenty people showed up at their first meeting, the "Harmonicoots" group — the Coots, for short — was born. For the seven years since then, the Coots — sixty men and women over fifty-five — have met weekly with three goals: having fun, learning new songs, and playing together.

They have since played more than 250 gigs in retirement homes, hospitals, parades, elementary schools, and churches, often bringing tears to grateful listeners. The Coots now have a mission to "entice the world" to the joys of playing, inspiring and exciting young and old to a lifetime of musical enjoyment. They've helped hospital residents improve their breathing capacity, and they've played carols on harmonica over the holidays. Some of the members have traveled worldwide.

What began as a postretirement whim turned into a new calling — and could have also become a late-blooming career, except that Bud and the Coots use any income they make to purchase harmonicas that they donate to elementary school students. Thanks to the Coots, these students enjoy a fresh breath of life.

This final story relates how a young man followed a call to accomplish something great against all odds.

In 2001, during a severe drought in his village in Malawi, fourteen-year-old William Kamkwamba was forced to drop out of school because his family couldn't afford the tuition. It was all they could do to sustain themselves on one meal a day from their meager farm income.

Young William spent his time in a nearby library, fascinated by a book on windmills. Not knowing any better, he believed that he could build a windmill for his village, assembled from old car batteries, bike parts, tractor fans, and plastic pipes. Spent wood from local blue-gum trees would serve as a tower. His parents and everyone else thought he'd lost his reason, but their doubt only increased this young man's determination.

Three months later, William illuminated his family's home with a lightbulb powered by his first windmill. He later built four more in his village, including one at a local school where he taught others how to build windmills. This resulted in electricity for the village, which enabled them to pump in their own water — a gift that became a village treasure.

William's story and the stories that preceded it are but a tiny sampling among millions of stories of career and calling, as interesting and varied as the people on our planet. Yet the most significant story is your own. Your personal memories are your treasures — and each story, each memory, can provide teachable moments.

It doesn't ultimately matter whether your career and calling are united or are two separate parts of your life. In an ideal world, career and calling might merge — we would feel drawn, as if from above, to do the work we do each day. But this is the real world, where not every calling becomes a career or every career a calling. Most of us go to work, put in our time, enjoy aspects of our job, then look forward to doing what we do for love alone during our discretionary time.

There are, after all, benefits in *not* centering your life around your career. When your work is "just a job" that you leave behind each evening, you aren't as likely to get overly stressed or define your worth by the work you do, even as you strive to do your work well. Your family may also benefit from the extra time, attention, and energy you have to spend with them.

The balance between career, calling, and family will naturally change over time, so reevaluating and fine-tuning this balance can help transform midlife crises into midcourse corrections and create a space for refueling and recharging. Maintaining such balance involves a process of self-examination and insight that ripens over time.

Self-Knowledge and Career Decisions

Thousands of years ago, the Athenian lawgiver Solon offered two words of guidance that have echoed through the ages: *Know thyself*. These words were inscribed in the forecourt of the Temple of Apollo at Delphi and also attributed to numerous sages, including Heraclites, Pythagoras, and Socrates (who proposed that "the unexamined life is not worth living"). Why would such sages recommend self-awareness above other human qualities? Perhaps it's because self-knowledge informs all our choices and decisions (in education, careers, and relationships) and thereby shapes the quality of our lives.

In high school and college we begin, by necessity, to learn something of our interests and capacities. We begin to sort out whether we're more of a workhorse or an innovator, and whether we lean toward science or liberal arts. But it can take time to discern what we really *want* to do as opposed to what we think we *should* do (to please parents or to garner status or respect).

If self-knowledge were easy or automatic, then most of us would make clear and wise decisions from our early years about schooling, career, mate, and so on. But all too often, through our twenties, our choices are ill-informed — a mixture of hope and guesswork. Jobs and relationships become a series of learning experiences as life doesn't work out as we might have hoped or planned. (If only we had known then what we know now...)

The majority of twenty-somethings leave college with limited self-knowledge, a bachelor's degree, and a big question: *Now what?* Throughout the "trying twenties" — when we try this, then try that — we strive to understand ourselves enough to find our place in the world.

Deciding on a Career

Decision making is a fundamental life skill, and (as with choosing a life partner) your career choice is one of life's major decisions. Decisions demand that you come to know yourself. Otherwise, you may make the right choice for the wrong person — the one you hoped or believed you were rather than the one you are.

There is no best career — only the best one for you at a given time of your life. There are both satisfied and dissatisfied people in medicine, plumbing, hairstyling, law, sales, teaching, and every other line of work. Life is an experiment, a laboratory of self-exploration. So, until you find a truly satisfying vocation, just get a job. Choose the best option available now. Meanwhile, stay open to new opportunities, until you find a career or calling you are ready to commit to for a significant period of time. Today, it's not unusual to go through several careers in the course of our working lives.

My Own Search

In my own search for a career and calling, I traveled a winding path. After college graduation, I sold life insurance in Los Angeles for two months, until I was offered a head coaching position at Stanford University; after four successful years, I was invited to join the faculty at Oberlin College. Professionally, it felt as if I was leading a charmed life — a head coach at twenty-two, then a college professor — until I decided to return to Berkeley to teach at a spiritual institute for six months.

Then my life changed considerably. I taught gymnastics part-time at the Berkeley YMCA (three months), went on unemployment (two months), nearly joined the Navy but ended up in a spiritual community (on and off, eight years), during which time I worked as a typist-secretary (was fired after four months), taught at a small gymnastics studio in San Francisco (six months), moved to Atlanta to coach a girls gymnastics team (nine months), attended graduate school in psychology in California (four months), started court reporting school in San Francisco (six months), taught a martial arts/acrobatics class at the Berkeley YMCA (three months), served as the women's gymnastics coach at UC Berkeley (two years), and returned to Oberlin College (two years), where my wife, Joy, served as dorm director and where I wrote the final draft of *Way of the Peaceful Warrior*. Soon after publication, the book went out of print — and I returned to the San Francisco Bay Area, where I found temporary work doing data entry for Bank of America, then spent the next eleven months word processing for a management firm before moving on to two typing jobs — one from 5 to 8:30 AM and another from 9 to 5. The long workdays lasted eight months, until I found an administrative position, which lasted a year.

Then, in 1983, I started my own personal fitness coaching business.

It wasn't until 1984, at age thirty-eight, when *Way of the Peaceful Warrior* was republished and word of mouth began to build, that I created some Peaceful Warrior audio programs and began teaching workshops. At last, I had found my career and calling — writing, teaching, and speaking.

They say it takes ten years to become an "overnight success." In my case it took sixteen years of experimentation and uncertainty — treading water until I learned to swim. So the observations I share are not abstract theories. I've been in the trenches; I've done the soul-searching, experienced the disorientation and doubt. Those years of searching were, in retrospect, a necessary period of introspection and self-inquiry.

On the quest to find our career and calling, we're like people driving in the dark — we can see only as far as our headlights illuminate. Meanwhile, the better we understand ourselves, the better we steer our course. That is why self-knowledge may be the heart of wisdom — and wisdom is earned over time.

Talents, Interests, and Values

The path to career and calling is like a treasure hunt — and at a crossroads where three key qualities intersect, you'll find a signpost pointing toward work you are most likely to find fulfilling. Those qualities can be expressed by three questions, the answers to which require time and experience to fully grasp: *What are my talents? What are my interests? What are my values?*

Talents

During my freshman year in college, I was preoccupied with women who didn't seem to know that I existed. I asked a few out until I finally got the message that they just weren't interested. Meanwhile, I tended to discount women who were friendly toward me. When I shared my situation with a teammate, he said something I never forgot: "Dan, some girls aren't going to like you no matter how much you try, and other girls are going to like you just as you are. Why waste your time on the ones who aren't that into you?"

That story and advice also apply to your career search. For any number of reasons, many people pursue work that doesn't match their talents, hoping to improve as they go — a little like buying a suit, then trying to tailor yourself to fit the clothing. There's nothing wrong with experimenting and trying different sorts of work, but why not pursue a career consistent with your innate talents and established abilities?

Some of us are stronger in sports or mathematics than in English or art, or the opposite may be true. As Will Rogers said, "We're all ignorant, only on different subjects." In searching for a career, we naturally want to learn all we can about the career, online and in the field — even interviewing those in a profession. But even more important, we have to "research ourselves." And one important part of self-knowledge follows from a realistic assessment of our strengths and weaknesses, revealed over time in the school of experience. This reminds me of a story:

I was about to catch the team bus to the gymnastics conference championships, where I would compete the next day, when I dropped by the old Texaco station. As soon as Socrates saw me, he beckoned me to come into the garage, where he handed me a heavy case of engine oil. I was asking him where he wanted me to put it when he said, "Just hold on to it for a minute" — and he placed a second case on top of the first one. I could barely hold both cases. Ignoring my strained expression, he then started piling individual cans of oil on top of the two cases in my shaking arms. "Socrates," I said, panting, "I can't —"

My arms collapsed, and the boxes and cans crashed to the floor at my feet. I stared down at them, then looked up at Socrates, whose expression revealed nothing. "Okay," I said. "This was some kind of a test, right? And I failed..."

When Socrates finished laughing at my sullen expression, he said, "Life is not about success or failure, Dan — it's about stretching yourself. How will you ever know your limits until you've tested them? And how do you test them unless you're willing to fail brilliantly?"

That competition the next day was one of the best of my life, because I tested my limits and discovered the truth of Soc's words. As playwright and orator George Bernard Shaw wrote, "I learned to speak as I learned to skate or cycle — by doggedly making a fool of myself until I got used to it."

Never assume limits until you've tested them. You may not lack talent; you may only lack experience. The impressions we form of our level of talent — even early on, as children — can be based on our far too limited exposure, or even a single incident. Years ago I watched as my daughter took a children's gymnastics class taught by a new instructor. He had the youngsters line up and told them it was time to learn cartwheels. He told them to hold up their arms, put one leg forward, then "kick over the top" and attempt a cartwheel. The children attempted one after another. My daughter, like some of the other children, did the cartwheels easily and well, because she had previous experience. But some of the children had never before attempted this movement and, as beginners, naturally fell down once, and again. This is where a skilled instructor would have given more helpful feedback for these beginners, but he could only tell them to "keep your head up and your arms straight." They fell again. As a parent, it was not my place to take over the class. I could only observe the frustration and disappointment on their little faces as the beliefs took shape that they weren't as talented as their classmates.

You've also formed assumptions about your talent (or lack of talent) in math or singing, cooking or sports, art or reading comprehension. Maybe those assumptions are correct — or maybe they're not. But if you're willing to apply yourself, even modest talent combined with effort over time can reap significant improvement. Still, you're more likely to invest your time and effort in an area of abiding interest.

In every field there are those with abundant talent who have little interest in a given arena — and others who have great interest but little talent. Of the two, interest in (or passion for) a given vocation may be the more important factor.

Interests

On the face of it, you'd think interest would be easy to determine. After all, you either have an interest in something or you don't. But your level of interest is often complicated by beliefs in your capacity in a given area — by your self-concept. For example, I became "less interested" in painting because I formed a mistaken belief that I wasn't much good at it. It happened like this:

I started kindergarten a week or two late due to a flu. On my first day I was given paint, a brush, and an easel and told to paint a tree. My tree looked like a green lollipop. Still, I was moderately pleased with my creation — until I compared it to those of the children around me, whose trees had branches and individual leaves. Unaware that the other children had been practicing painting trees nearly every day, I mistakenly concluded that I wasn't as good as the other students. So the next day, when I was given a choice to go paint pictures or to climb the monkey bars, you can guess which activity I chose. My interest in climbing grew along with my skills, and painting was all but abandoned. So due to a simple misunderstanding, I turned away from the path of art even as a future in gymnastics beckoned.

Added to this basic complication of (often distorted) self-concept influencing our interests, we spend much of our teens and twenties sorting out what we (or our parents or peers) think we *should* or *could* do from what we actually *like* doing. We can only guess at the number of misguided decisions that have turned someone away from an interest because they were told that it had "no future."

Many high achievers have been pushed to the top of their professional ladder by social pressures or parental expectations, only to discover later that the ladder was "leaning against the wrong wall." For example, I know two former attorneys who switched careers midstream — one began a long and successful career as the head swimming coach at Stanford University; the other became a respected sports chiropractor, whose clients include a major city ballet company and a professional sports team.

So consider carefully the kinds of areas or activities you genuinely enjoy — since interest is a clear guidepost at any career crossroads — which is why I advised my daughters, "Do what you love, then get someone to pay you for it."

Values

We humans cling to a variety of divergent values. Some of us, for example, have more puritan values (such as self-denial and delayed gratification) — we go with the rules. Others of us value a more hedonist lifestyle (valuing self-indulgence and immediate gratification) — we go with our impulses. Some lean toward the sentimental; others have a tougher, more rigid character. Still others embody the lone wolf or the social butterfly, the believer or the skeptic. These values, along with our interests and talents, all propel us along our career and life paths.

Your unique combination of values — what seems right, ethical, and worthwhile to you — is revealed in your choices and behavior. I don't mean to suggest that one set of values is better than another. Remember the rules in the school of life — it's not about right or wrong, but about choices and consequences.

Your Core Value

On the path to self-knowledge, in the arena of career and calling it's important to know which of three criteria, or values, is most important to you: location, relationship, or career. Most of us appreciate that all three are important — but if you had to pick a core value and subordinate (or sacrifice) the other two, which might that be? Reflecting on your life and choices, you may realize that one has taken precedence over other areas on your personal scale of values. Let's consider a few brief examples.

Location: Rebecca's star is hitched to Boulder, Colorado, a city that captures her imagination. Centered on that location, she's set on moving there. Once she settles in, she'll then meet people and find whatever work she can, but for her, the people and work are secondary priorities.

Relationship: Jason is a carpenter and can work anywhere. His partner, just completing an internship, is applying to a number of medical residency programs. Jason is committed to the love of his life, around which all else revolves. Home for him is where the heart is, wherever his love may go. He's committed to a person more than any given place, and he'll find work wherever he goes.

Career: Elizabeth is devoted to her work, the central value in her life, where she derives the strongest sense of purpose and meaning. She will go to whatever location best serves her career and develop a circle of friends there in the free time her work allows.

WE EACH HAVE DIFFERENT VALUES and make our choices accordingly. Some years ago, a friend and fellow professor at a college in the Midwest lived on campus, while her husband worked as a government attorney on the West Coast. They loved each other dearly. She flew to visit him every few weeks, and he did the same for her. But their work (and necessary locations) took priority over living together — a mutual choice based on their values and circumstances.

Our values of place, people, or work are not necessarily fixed for life; they can change over time. If, for example, Boulder-loving Rebecca meets the love of her life and that person is offered a wonderful career opportunity in another state, then Rebecca may need to reexamine her core value.

In literature, in film, and in life, *character and values are revealed by choices people make under pressure.* Self-knowledge — in this case, knowing your central value — helps you to make clear decisions, even as the decisions you make also add to your inventory of self-knowledge. As E. M. Forster wrote, "How do I know what I think until I see what I do?"

Career Criteria: The Trinity of Needs

Knowing your core value is only one facet of self-knowledge and career choice. You also need to measure any potential career against three essential key criteria: *Do I find the work satisfying? Can I make good money? Does it provide a useful service?* These questions point to the three essential components of a fulfilling work life. Two out of the three may seem sufficient for a while, but all three elements are usually required in a satisfying long-term career. And (along with unfair or incompetent superiors or repressive company policies) the lack of one or more of these three basic elements is the primary cause of dissatisfaction and complaints in the workplace.

Satisfying Work

In America and elsewhere during the Great Depression of the 1930s, hungry men and women would travel if necessary and do virtually any work they could (preferably legal) to earn a few dollars. My father grew into adulthood during those difficult years. When I once asked him whether his work made him happy, he looked puzzled for a moment, then replied, "It never occurred to me." For him, happiness was not part of the career equation. His goal was supporting his family in the best way he knew how.

Many immigrants today also do whatever work is available — they don't likely ponder whether the work fits their aesthetic sensibilities. Yet they derive a sense of meaning and purpose from being able to support their families and seek better opportunities for their children.

The same is true for many people in the world today. But those of us who do have a wider array of work options and opportunities — thanks to the labors of our parents and grandparents, and better education and skills — are able to carefully consider the issue of "right livelihood" and to seek work that matches our talents, interests, and values.

There is no best vocation — only the most suitable for a given individual. Some kinds of work entail more physical exertion and skills, and other kinds involve more mental labor; certain careers require contact with the public, and others call for solitude; and some select professions confer higher status or social recognition than other jobs. We can find people who enjoy every sort of position. Zen and Taoist literature is full of enlightened butchers and wise craftspeople, and long ago there was that carpenter from Nazareth who also found a higher calling.

What you do matters, but *how* you do it matters even more. *Fulfillment lies not in the work itself but in the quality and care you bring to it.* Those who take pride in the quality of their work, no matter how humble, experience a meditative absorption that makes time fly, and that in itself can be fulfilling.

In Japan years ago, while waiting on a train platform for the bullet train, I observed a railroad employee cleaning one of hundreds of silver posts supporting a long railing that ran the entire length of the platform. He polished the posts, devoting about thirty seconds to each, making sure it was shining and spotless before moving on to the next. The man showed the concentration of a Zen master as he moved gracefully through his task, absorbed in his work. Few of us would consider polishing posts creative or satisfying work, and perhaps it wasn't what this man had dreamed of doing as a child. But from what I observed, the pride he took made his efforts a work of art. In a sense he was also polishing his spirit.

So bear in mind that you don't only *find* a fulfilling career; you create it — like that Zen master on the railway platform.

Good Money

What you or I may consider a "good income" will differ, depending on our skills, experience, and circumstances. But in each case, the compensation must feel fair, appropriate to the work, and sufficient to meet our needs. Otherwise, unless you are either a masochist or a saint, you're unlikely to tolerate underpayment over time.

There are, of course, other forms of compensation besides monetary income. You may accept work offering minimum pay but exceedingly pleasant surroundings or medical or other benefits, or because you believe in your employer's mission.

A woman I'll call Jean came to work for me part-time some years ago. She was decompressing from a high-paying, high-pressure job with a software start-up company in Silicon Valley. On the verge of burnout after working weeknights and weekends, she'd read our small announcement for part-time work and contacted us. Jean had read a few of my books and was thrilled to be able to work in a relaxed, informal, and positive atmosphere; reclaim some personal space; rebalance her life; and reset her priorities. Her delight with the work never wavered, but after about six months, she had to move on again — in her words, to "find better-paying, full-time work more suitable to her 'market value.'" We wished her well in finding the middle ground she sought, a position that would meet her financial needs without undue pressure or demands.

Useful Service

I've known only two people who made good money doing satisfying work but whose labors performed no useful service for anyone. One of them was a criminal; the other was a professional poker player. (Some people suggest that making a distinction between the two is splitting hairs, but I respectfully disagree.) Both were takers, however, who left a trail of sorrow and frustration behind them. The first man is currently incarcerated — he got tired of running. The other may still be sitting in a card room somewhere, patiently doing his professional best to take other people's money. He enjoys many aspects of his work and makes a good living, but he once confessed that he felt isolated — a lone wolf who wondered if "something was missing" from his life, like a sense of service and connection, a way to help make the world a better place. And to the extent we do provide a service, we experience a connection and meaning intimately connected to true fulfillment.

Not everyone is going to become a life-saving neurosurgeon or great philanthropist or celebrated master artist. Most of us do our jobs without fanfare or wide recognition. We assist and labor in stores and small businesses, in corporate buildings and markets and shops and gardens, doing work no less important than that of the rich and famous. But how many of us take ourselves and our skills for granted? How few of us appreciate the important service we provide?

Most people think of "service" as volunteering for the needy, helping with charities, or delivering food to the elderly or homebound. Such acts are certainly commendable. Yet someone who helps assemble furnaces or automobiles or televisions, making sure that every part fits, that every screw is tight, and that the construction is top quality, provides a significant service on whose skills others depend.

It's easy to devalue the worth of our work if we provide a less-creative service like doing data entry or answering phones in a small office or large corporation. But such work connects us with others and helps our world function. We are all links in the chain, and every link counts — even the criminal and the poker player, who also eventually learn what they need in life's continuing education.

THESE THREE ESSENTIAL CRITERIA — doing satisfying work, making a good income, and offering a useful service — provide another facet of self-knowledge that leads to better-informed decisions, and point us toward a fulfilling and sustainable career.

Career Decisions: Analysis and Imagination

Most of us have grown up in a world that places the highest value on logic, analysis, and the scientific method.

Yet *nearly all scientific discoveries and breakthroughs arise from our imaginative and intuitive faculties* (only to be later tested and validated through experiment and analysis).

Few of us find a career through logic, however — more often we find work through personal or secondary connections and sometimes through sheer coincidence. Here's a personal example: I left Berkeley and moved back to Los Angeles with my pregnant wife and an undergraduate degree in psychology. Since we had less than $500 remaining in our account, I searched through the want ads and found work as a trainee at a local office of New England Life Insurance. I got the job, bought a suit, and did my best to sell life insurance products. After two months I knew two things: First, that selling insurance might be perfect for some people, but it wasn't for me; second, I needed to move out of Los Angeles and back to the San Francisco Bay Area. So I quit the job, drove up to Sacramento, where I dropped off my wife to visit with her parents for a few days, and from there drove the two hours down to Berkeley to explore my options, thinking that with my background I might find work as a recreation director or something similar. I stopped by the office of my old coach to say hello and let him know I was looking for a job. He said, "Good timing, Dan — I just heard this morning that the Stanford [gymnastics] coaching job opened up yesterday — why don't you go speak with the athletic director?" I did so — and the next day I was hired as the head gymnastics coach at Stanford University.

I may have found that job through timing and luck — but it was preceded by years of intensive training in the field, confirming that luck happens when preparation meets opportunity. I hadn't been looking for a college coaching job, and I didn't find it through reason or analysis. In fact, logic is not well suited for making career decisions, because our analytical brain can only weigh variables — pros and cons, benefits and liabilities — trying to sort out a reasonable course of action. Doing so can generate for many people a state of "paralysis by analysis."

Have you ever made a rational decision, then awakened in the night or the next morning feeling uneasy about that choice without knowing why? It may be wise to pay attention to your intuitive sense regarding any important decision. Ideally, you want to use both imagination and reason in any problem-solving task — just not necessarily at the same time. Reason reflects an intellectual skill of the conscious mind; intuition reflects the deeper grasp of the subconscious mind, which sends messages to the conscious mind in various ways, including dreams.

During my tenure as the Stanford coach, one of the gymnasts on our team shared an assignment he was given that brought home the power and value of the subconscious mind in problem solving. Ted told me about a strange riddle he'd been assigned earlier that day in Dr. William Dement's Sleep and Dreaming course. The entire riddle consisted of eight letters: H-I-J-K-L-M-N-O. Ted didn't have a clue what it was about. His assignment was to ruminate on the riddle before going to sleep, with the intention of solving it — even if he didn't understand it — then to write down his dreams when he awoke the next day. Ted came to the gym the next morning and told me he'd written down his dreams but still had no clue about the riddle's meaning or solution. He showed me his dream notes — images of an old sailing ship in a stormy sea, with waves crashing and rain pouring down in torrents. It made no sense at all — until Ted learned the answer to the riddle and realized that his subconscious mind had indeed solved it beautifully, all without any conscious clue about what was going on. The riddle, H-I-J-K-L-M-N-O, was composed of the letters H to O, or H_2O, the chemical symbol for water, images of which had filled Ted's dreams.

Years later, as a writer, I experienced a similar phenomenon again and again. After I had written myself into a corner and the plot line was stuck, or I didn't know where to go next with a particular train of thought, I'd sleep on it — and, as often as not, the solution would pop into my head upon waking the next morning.

Time Travel with Your Subconscious Mind

The following method enables you to engage both your conscious and subconscious mind to make a better-informed decision about career (or any other facet of life). In a way, you're about to experience a form of time travel that engages your imaginative capacities in any decision-making process.

With practice, this time-travel process becomes simple and straightforward, and it represents an investment of just ten to fifteen minutes. You simply let your imagination travel through time. This process can help you choose the best of two, three, four, or more options. But for the sake of presenting the process, let's say someone's choosing between A and B.

Examples are Kristen deciding between two colleges; Mahmoud weighing whether to look for work in his current city, where his girlfriend lives, or to accept a good job overseas; and Maliha considering the offers of two admirers who have both proposed to her. Or there's Caleb and his start-up software company, which is beginning to take off, and he can either expand or accept a buyout from a software giant; Samantha can accept a high-paying corporate accounting job or start her own firm; Curtis has to choose whether to undergo expensive, high-risk surgery, chemotherapy, and radiation or settle his affairs and let go; and Sarah must decide whether to take an early-retirement package and minimum Social Security payments or to push on for a few more years so she'll receive maximum Social Security benefits.

The decision you face may be similar to or quite different from the examples above, but the process is the same. So here's the time-travel exercise.

1. Choose A. Settle into the idea that you have *fully* committed to A. This step is essential.

2. Ask yourself this three-part question:

    Having committed to A, What will I be doing, what will I be feeling, and what will I look like *one hour from now?*

    Ideally, write down the answers to the three parts of the question. Your answers may be brief, but write them down. At the very least, imagine the answers vividly. See what comes up. It's not likely to be too difficult to imagine one hour from now.

3. Ask yourself the same three-part question, but instead of *one hour from now*, imagine *one day from now*. Again, write down the responses that come up.

4. Same three-part question, but imagine *one month from now*.

5. Same three-part question, but imagine *one year from now*.

6. Same three-part question, but imagine *ten years from now*. At this point, you may feel like saying, "Wait a minute. How can I possibly know what I'll be doing, be feeling, and look like (having committed to A) a decade hence? That's just my imagination." Right. It's your imagination — a bridge to intuitive sight. After all, why do you imagine one thing and not another?

When this process is complete, repeat it for option B. That is, say to yourself, "What was I thinking? Clearly, B is the best choice!" And commit to that. Feel into it. You have chosen B. Now go through all the steps just mentioned.

When you've written down (and/or vividly imagined) all your responses for both A and B (and C, if there's a third option), you will have transformed tunnel vision into a more expansive, intuitive depth and breadth of vision. This doesn't mean you will now have absolute certainty, but you'll be better prepared to make a firm decision.

Deciding to Decide

Most of us view a decision as a mental process and conclusion — but in fact, no decision becomes real until one acts on it. This became clear to me some years ago, while I was on a solo hike in the high Sierra. I was heading back to camp as the sun sank toward the crest of a peak, when I came to a fork in the road. I wasn't sure which path to take. I peered ahead, examined the terrain, and weighed my options. First the right fork looked more promising; then I changed my mind and leaned toward the left, until my intuition urged me again to the right. This indecision continued as azure sky turned a darker shade. I decided left; I decided right — but I made no progress until I took action and started down one path.

Decide to decide — and when you act, do so with the full force of your being. Second-guessing yourself is a form of self-abuse. As Zen master Ummon reminded his students, "When you sit, sit; when you stand, stand — just don't wobble between the two!"

Remain committed to whatever course you've chosen unless you get new and compelling reasons to change course. If you've committed to cross a rushing mountain stream only to realize a third of the way across that the current is too swift and deep for a safe crossing, a change of plans may be not only appropriate but wise. The same is true in your larger life. If you're staying in an abusive relationship or punishing job, it may be time to reconsider and recommit to a more life-affirming direction, taking into account your boundaries, rights, and worth. (There's a difference between commitment and masochism.)

However, for most decisions we make, even as doubts and difficulties arise, commitment means marching forward, persisting through challenges, and keeping faith in yourself and in your course of action. *Faith is the courage to live as if everything that happens, and every choice we make, is for our highest good and learning.* Faith is also nourished by the higher understanding that every decision eventually leads to wisdom.

Career Notes: From Entry Level to Leadership

Any insight into our second purpose — career and calling — must include a look at the roles we play in the evolving cycles of our lives at work. I've experienced entry level and also played a leadership role; so have you — at home, at work, or in the larger world. Every time we face some new task or responsibility, we experience the entry-level challenges, the beginner's mind. And leadership turns out to be more about a personal set of qualities than a position of power, corner office, or company title. You will soon discover how it's possible to demonstrate qualities of leadership even at entry level, or any stage of your personal career arc.

Now it's time to address key facets upon which our work experience will turn.

Committing to Excellence: You may have a number of careers or callings in the course of your life. But no matter what your tasks and duties appear to be, committing to excellence and quality adds meaning and value to your days. For example, some years ago, I was supporting my family by working two jobs: overload typing at a law firm early in the mornings, followed by data entry at a real estate firm the rest of the day. Not the most creative of duties, nor my long-term choice of careers, but the best employment I could find at the time. So I aimed to be an excellent data-entry person. I look back on that period without regret (and with some pride), because I provided high-quality work for my employer until it was time to move on.

Rungs on the Career Ladder: Why is it that some of us move up the ladder, while others are content with lower-level positions, and still others work for themselves? We might as well ask why some athletes become Olympians and others enjoy the junior varsity — or why some people work behind the camera and others in front of it. If we did ask why, we might come up with factors including genetics, birth order, life experience, beliefs and self-concept, educational opportunities, socioeconomic status, role models, friends and networks, family support, energy level, drive, talent, intelligence, exposure, location, the state of the economy, and a measure of chance or destiny.

Your own unique combination of such factors may direct you to a subordinate position or drive you upward to the rarified air and higher pressures of a top-floor corner office.

Those who ascend to the peaks may, or may not, be happier or more satisfied than those who live down in the valleys. The main thing is to find the most suitable work you can (keeping in mind the criteria we've already covered) while staying open to new opportunities. Your career is not a marriage; you don't have to make a lifetime commitment to your employer (any more than your employer makes such a commitment to

77

you). So there's nothing wrong with staying apprised of opportunities in your field or another that may better fit your talents, values, and interests.

Two Secrets of Success for the Self-Employed: I sometimes tell people that I have an extremely demanding boss — and I'm self-employed. If you're in a similar situation, note the two key factors that will enhance your chances of success: 1. *Be good at what you do*; and 2. *be good at promoting what you do* (or hire someone who will do that for you). If you have good skills but fall short at marketing yourself, keep in mind that your business can only serve people who know that you exist.

Your Leadership Qualities

I learned about leadership skills and responsibilities in the field, while coaching college athletes. I needed to set high standards, provide feedback, motivate and support team members, troubleshoot when necessary, and create a productive environment that encouraged innovation — the same responsibilities taken on by CEOs, high-level managers, politicians, parents, coaches, teachers, and leaders in any walk of life.

No matter what role you play at work or at home, you influence people around you — you teach and lead by example — because people notice what you do. Therefore, leadership is a universal calling that has nothing to do with one's status or level of authority in an organization. Tyrants, dictators, and despots may be powerful rulers yet poor leaders. One can serve as chairman of the board but lack essential leadership skills, while someone who works in the mail room inspires others to quality work. Many of us play a leadership role in our circle of family or friends.

So what are the key qualities of an effective leader? As you read the following, consider how you (might) demonstrate these qualities among your friends, loved ones, and colleagues.

As a leader you inspire by example. Humanitarian-physician Albert Schweitzer once said, "In influencing other people, example is not the main thing; it is the only thing." You embody the qualities that you'd like to see in others.

As a leader you offer support where needed. People don't care how much you know unless they also know how much you care. Support means setting the bar high, then asking, "How can I help you accomplish this goal?"

As a leader you motivate by pointing out a higher purpose. You transform a job into a service-oriented mission, incorporating meaningful, big-picture goals into the work at hand. You present tasks not as an end in themselves but as a means of personal growth, lifting the game to another level.

As a leader you appreciate the value of mistakes. You understand that mistakes can lead to breakthroughs, to new insight and innovation. So true leaders encourage risk and accept new and creative errors in the process of learning and growth.

As a leader you encourage collaboration rather than competition. Competition for external rewards, perks, and bonuses results in workers who feel like rats running for food pellets — but "the problem with the rat race," quipped actress Lily Tomlin, "is that even if you win you're still a rat." And highly competitive environments are often described as "soul-killing" by those caught in the maze. The competitive spirit that stimulates short-term drive among high achievers can also lead to burn-out and resentment. In contrast, a spirit of collaboration — when one person's contribution (supported by others) reflects well on the entire team — generates a connected, productive, and friendly workplace where open systems and information sharing replace self-protective strategies.

As a leader you empower others. You become a bridge over which others may cross. You remind your team that *no one is smarter than all of us* — and you focus on what's right, not who's right. Using not only the brains you have but all you can borrow, you shift the focus from "What's in it for me?" to "What serves the highest good of all concerned?"

How Will You Spend Your Life?

Contemplate for a moment the mysterious aspects of how you ended up where you are now. Consider the open road ahead, which, like any good novel, may bring surprising twists and turns. As you grow stronger and wiser through the hurdles you meet along the way, hold to the faith that your life is unfolding as it should — that every bump in the road is a part of your unique process. Treasure your career and calling, no matter how humble; trust the changing rhythms of your life, shaped by the talents, interests, and values you hold dear.

Our discussion of the second purpose of life — *finding your career and calling* — opened with a reminder about the hours we are given each day. Now we return to this central issue and close with some big-picture perspectives about your life and work.

The hours of your life are the most valuable currency you will ever have. How will you spend them?

Imagine winning a huge lottery — you'd never again need to work for money. What then would you do with your time? How would you spend your life? Would you give of your time and talent in creative service to the world? Or would you pursue amusements, pleasures, traveling, and celebrity, collecting sensory experiences and possessions, playing with power and status and influence? Let's suppose that "billionaire you" bought everything you've ever wanted. Then you traveled around the world on the finest cruises and stayed at luxury hotels. You acquired beautifully furnished homes with staff in numerous prime locations. If you became bored or restless in one place, you'd take your private jet to another — and buy (or have your personal assistant purchase) all the cars and toys and clothing you could want and the best schools for your children.

Then what? Would you preview the newest movies on the biggest screens? Play video games day after day? Arrange for one sensory pleasure after another? Be seen with the rich and famous? And *then* what? Entertainments and amusements can distract almost anyone from a sense of emptiness — at least for a while. But when our life nears its end, what do we want to look back on? So the question remains for us each to answer for ourselves: Can a self-pleasuring life lead to genuine fulfillment? The following tale addresses this perennial question.

A thief named Willy, making his escape from a high-rise penthouse, falls from the fire escape toward certain death thirty-five floors below. A moment later, it seems, he finds himself in a fancy pool hall, in perfect physical shape. Willy concludes that he has died and gone to heaven — because pool is his all-time favorite hobby. With a sense of relief and joy, he racks up and discovers he has somehow become a master at the game. His only regret is that no one else can see his triumph in this empty establishment as he sinks one shot after another.

Later that day as he explores his new environment, he visits a swimming pool and finds himself performing Olympic-caliber dives from the three-meter board, then cutting through the water in what must be record time. At a nearby casino, where he meets taciturn croupiers and silent dealers, he starts with a few dollars in his pocket and emerges a millionaire — the luckiest man alive. He finds a hotel and pays in advance for a month in the executive suite. The next day is a blissful repeat of the day before. He races cars, wins another fortune at video poker, and beds six gorgeous women, having discovered a profound new virility.

It's an amazing week, and a pretty good month, but as time passes, Willy begins to tire of the constant winning and his mastery of everything and everyone. Within six months he feels like he's going mad. He undertakes a search for St. Peter or whoever's in charge, so he can express his dissatisfaction. After an exhausting search he finally reaches the main administration hall. An efficient secretary waves him into a grand office, where he finds a well-dressed man sitting behind a massive mahogany desk. "May I help you?" asks the official.

With that, Willy begins a litany of complaints: the terrible boredom, the effortless success and victory at every turn, ending with, "I never thought that heaven would be anything like this."

The official stands slowly, and his eyes reflect a reddish glow. "What," he asks, "makes you think that this is heaven?"

The wealthiest and most privileged among us may have special appreciation for Willy's dilemma, because no matter how many moments of self-gratification money can buy, fulfillment eludes us until we find meaning, purpose, and connection. Indeed, a growing number of billionaires today find that meaning by donating a significant share of their wealth in service of others, and celebrities find worthy causes, using their fame for a higher purpose.

Years ago I met a woman I'll call Doris who had hundreds of millions of dollars from a family trust. When I first met her, she fit my image of a "spoiled rich girl." She seemed to possess a sense of self-importance but not a lot of personality. She made no effort to be kind or even courteous. Perhaps from her view she didn't need to observe social niceties. She ignored the live-in staff as they cleaned and gardened. She deigned to speak with me only because, being an avid reader, she had enjoyed some of my books.

Doris was not an easy person to like. At that time I had no knowledge that she was desperately unhappy in her relationship and dissatisfied with her life. Only years later did I find out that several months after our meeting, and after a difficult divorce, she had made two significant changes in her life: First, Doris set up a philanthropic foundation to help others in need; second, she found regular part-time work in a small flower shop. She had always loved flowers and now had a way to provide a direct, person-to-person service. Doris had created new meaning and purpose in her life, and a heartfelt connection with the larger world.

Unlike Doris, many millions of people on this planet are born into poverty. Their day-to-day lives are fully occupied with finding food and shelter. As Mohandas Gandhi put it, "To a starving man, God is bread." Yet despite, and even because of, their struggle for the bare necessities, many of the poorest among us have a clear sense of meaning, purpose, and connection as they cling together for the common good, doing their best to care for their families and communities.

The same call to service applies to retirees with

discretionary funds and time, who may at first pursue leisure activities, luxuriating in their new freedom. But for many, unlimited leisure becomes an endless "long weekend." So, echoing the search of young college graduates (and even the independently wealthy), retirees also confront the need to reexamine their current values, interests, and skills. Some go back to part-time work — not only for income but as a means to feel useful, reestablish personal or professional contacts, reaffirm their sense of relevance, or join a larger mission. And like younger people who may change jobs several times, retirees may also explore different ways to best serve, whether mentoring, consulting in a field of expertise, or working retail a few hours a day (as Doris did). So the paths of poverty, wealth, and even retirement can all lead to service.

The film *Groundhog Day* relates the story of Phil, a cynical television weather forecaster caught in an existential time loop while on a location shoot in Punxsutawney, Pennsylvania — he awakens every morning to the same day in the same town. He is the only character aware that he's living the same day over and over. At first he tries exploiting his knowledge, taking advantage of people and circumstance. As the endless repetition of days continues, he grows distraught and commits suicide again and again in a variety of ways, hoping for escape, but immediately awakens to yet another same day. Eventually, having explored every experience and exhausted all other options, Phil stops fighting and begins to improve himself — to study and practice piano, medicine, and other skills — until he finally realizes the ultimate lesson: There's nothing left to do but to serve, to become a useful force in the world. With this recognition, he finds his purpose (and love and salvation).

Groundhog Day represents our own evolutionary journey of awakening. As we come to appreciate how the world has supported us, fed us, taught us, and tested us — whether or not we earned these blessings or seem to deserve such grace — the call to service awakens. As my friend Lou, who sells life insurance and provides financial advice, told me, "I just use my work as an excuse to connect with people, to offer some kind and helpful words. Maybe we do some business, and maybe we don't. I hope their lives are richer for it; I know that mine is, for the wealth of friends I've made." Lou had realized what most of us are discovering — that we can't serve others without also elevating ourselves.

As you consider the arc of your career and the challenges of moving through the low points and difficulties that come with the territory, recall the first of the four purposes — learning life's lessons. You've learned much so far, and will continue to adapt and grow, mature and evolve. And during those times you feel stuck, stagnant, or even that you're slipping backward, you may actually be backing up to get a running start. So persist. Stand up for yourself. Lead by example. Practice the quiet courage of everyday life.

> *You have a sacred calling;*
> *The question is, will you*
> *take the time to heed that call?*
> *Will you blaze your own path?*
> *You are the author of your own life. . . .*
> *Don't let others define it for you.*
> *Real power comes by doing*
> *what you are meant to be doing,*
> *and doing it well.*

— OPRAH WINFREY

Your work — the service you provide, no matter how humble it may be — connects you to the larger community. So never take your work, or yourself, for granted. Author Leo Buscaglia reminded us all that "small acts of caring can turn a life around." One life you will turn around, through career and calling, is your own.

The Third Purpose

DISCOVERING YOUR LIFE PATH

- *Understand Your Hidden Calling*
- *Follow Your Higher Potential*

The shoe that fits one person pinches another;
there is no recipe for living that suits all cases.
Each of us carries our own life-plan,
which cannot be superseded by any other.

— C. G. JUNG

THUS FAR WE'VE EXPLORED the geography of the school of life, then cast off and sailed into the changing currents of career and calling — key areas on the surface of our lives. Now it's time to submerge into the depths. According to philosopher Søren Kierkegaard, "At birth we set sail into the world with sealed orders." In this, the third purpose of life, you'll gain access to those "sealed orders" and delve into your hidden calling, or life path.

The third purpose begins with the precept that we are each climbing a mountain toward our highest potential but by differing paths. Because few of us can see the drives, challenges, and gifts on our own life path from the valley of ordinary awareness, I present core elements of the Life-Purpose System — a method first detailed in my book *The Life You Were Born to Live*. This system provides a numeric key to the third purpose you are here to fulfill.

Hidden Calling, Higher Potential

Comprehending the third purpose requires an open mind and curious heart, because it introduces a system, drawn from an ancient mystical tradition, that doesn't easily lend itself to scientific explanation. Yet its accuracy points to unsolved mysteries and unexplored territory awaiting further study.

How I Discovered the Life-Purpose System

Despite nearly twenty years spent exploring the human psyche, various insight traditions, and metaphysical models of reality, I remain an empiricist at heart. I value the scientific method, which utilizes well-designed (double-blind, controlled) experiments to test whether a theory or hypothesis is in fact true — whether, for example, a medication, herb, or other substance works better than a placebo (sugar pill). The methods of science helped to pull humanity out of the dark ages of superstition. So over the years I've been skeptical of magical or wishful thinking and untested notions.

I hadn't even considered the existence of a deeper

calling, or anything like a "life path," until 1984, when I met an unusual mentor whom I'll refer to as MB. He had read my first book, *Way of the Peaceful Warrior*, and had decided to take me under his wing.

Not long after our initial encounter, MB sat me down and gave me a "reading," which changed the course of my life. In that session, he revealed in-depth information that clarified my past, present, and potential future, including details that rang true and proved amazingly accurate. It was as if his words removed a veil that had previously obscured my vision, and awakened in me the first clear recognition of the life I was born to live.

I was astonished that he could have such insight into my life but had no idea how he gained access to such information. I was at that time well versed in the "cold-read" techniques and tricks used by so-called psychics. MB claimed no psychic abilities, however, stating only that he had been trained to know "where to look" for such information. He would say no more about it at that time.

In the months that followed that session, I began to learn life's lessons with greater ease and openness, and to engage with life in a more assertive way. Understanding what I was here to do, I set out to do it. My family's financial situation improved correspondingly as I refined an approach to living that I called the *peaceful warrior's way*.

Meanwhile, I remained fascinated with MB's apparent intuitive abilities. So when he announced an advanced training he was offering in Hawaii, where he would teach, among other things, the basic elements of the system that gave him such uncanny insight into people's lives, I was the first to sign up. I could hardly believe that I might learn to do for other people what he had done for me.

At the training, I sat with about twenty other participants as MB began a series of lectures on this mysterious system. The first thing he revealed was an objective method of adding up the digits of anyone's date of birth, and then deriving meanings that provided insight into their lives.

I was initially disappointed by this revelation, as when a magician shows how a wondrous illusion is accomplished with mirrors and sleight of hand; the "magic" vanished. Besides, using people's birth dates sounded like numerology, an occult art that had never attracted me. It made no sense that adding the digits of someone's date of birth could yield accurate information about central issues in that person's life.

MB went on to explain that such methods had been

passed down in various cultures over the centuries, but that they differed in interpretations and degrees of accuracy. He added, "Once you learn more about this approach, you can determine for yourself the validity of the system." He then spent several evenings presenting information that pinpointed key issues in each of our lives.

The life path, or hidden calling, that you are about to explore points to what you are *really* here to fulfill — the innate drives, challenges, and gifts that for most people remain unseen or obscure.

I took careful notes from MB's lectures, outlining in about twenty pages the fundamental elements of the system. As soon as I returned home, I began to give free life-purpose readings to family and friends, using the basic information in my notes. Within a few weeks I had internalized the information and no longer needed any notes. Eventually, after working with many hundreds of people, my insight deepened and expanded.

Eight years later, I trained a small number of therapists, health professionals, and life coaches in the fundamentals of what I came to call the Life-Purpose System, and eventually I went on to write *The Life You Were Born to Live*.

Here, in the context of the four purposes of life, I present core elements of this system as a means to help you clarify your life path and hidden calling — the third purpose of life.

Determining Your Birth Number

You can choose either of two methods to determine your birth number, the key to your life path. The first is the quicker and more accurate.

Method One: Use the Life-Purpose Calculator Online

1. Go to www.peacefulwarrior.com using your computer, smart phone, or other electronic device with access to the Internet.

2. Click on the Life Purpose link to access the Life-Purpose Calculator.

3. Input your year, month, and day of birth. You will then see your birth number, along with a paragraph of summary information about your life path. Make note of your birth number before returning to this book.

Method Two: Do the Math

If you don't have access to the Internet, turn to the Appendix at the end of this book (page 151) for instructions on doing the math yourself. Once you have your birth number, make note of it and read on.

Your Birth Number and the Third Purpose

Like most people living today, you have a three-digit or four-digit birth number (or, like a small percentage of people born on certain dates after the year 2000, you might have a single-digit birth number).

You will soon learn the meanings and significance of the digits 1 through 9 as they relate to the challenges on your life path. Every digit in your birth number provides information and insight into your life path. However, please make note of the following.

- If you have a *three-digit* birth number (e.g., 27/9), then the final digit, to the right of the slash, represents your hidden calling — the third purpose you're here to fulfill.

- If you have a *four-digit* birth number (e.g., 29/11), then each of the two middle digits of your birth number (on either side of the slash) represents key elements of your third purpose.

- If you have a rare one-digit birth number, then that single digit alone represents your third purpose.

- A zero in your birth number (for example 20/2 or 28/10) indicates potential spiritual gifts, such as empathy, strength, or intuitive discernment.

- As you mature along your life path, the qualities associated with your birth number tend to evolve over time from more negative (less mature) aspects into more positive (constructive) forms.

To make sense of all these numbers and principles — bringing them down to earth and into your life — we now turn to the primary meanings and issues associated with each digit (1 through 9).

The Nine Life Paths

Study each of the following descriptions through the filter of your own history and experience, paying special attention to the digits of your birth number. And remember that each of the following life paths or callings (associated with the digits 1 through 9) represents primary drives and challenges.

1: Creativity

The 1 centers around creative energy — in the arts (writing, visual media, acting, music), or in education, business, family and childrearing, or any other field where creativity gives birth to new directions, solutions, or approaches. The 1 also indicates a knack for inventiveness or reinvention. When those with 1 (or double 1) in their birth number tackle their innate insecurity — an underlying sense of inferiority and driving need to prove themselves — and stop trying to fit in, then their creativity flows like a surging river. But creative energy is a double-edged sword; it can manifest in positive, productive, constructive forms or in negative or destructive ways (such as abuse or addiction). Physical exercise helps those working 1 energy to stay grounded and balanced. Applied in the positive, their energy charms, attracts, and inspires others to their own creative endeavors.

2: Cooperation

The 2 represents a drive to, and issues around, cooperative service but also a tendency to overcooperate, or start a relationship by overhelping, sometimes to the point of servitude — giving and giving (whether or not anyone asked) — then later resenting and resisting, withdrawing (physically or emotionally), feeling taken for granted. Those with 2 in their birth number (like those with 4) can feel overly responsible and take on responsibility to solve problems ("I'll just do it myself!"), and need to delegate at times. A key for those with 2 involves establishing a balance (and boundaries) between the needs (and responsibilities) of others and their own. Those working 2 can be strong and supportive worker bees, nurturers, and caregivers of the world. While fully capable of leading, their deepest and most satisfying calling is bringing loyal, capable support to a person, organization, or mission in service of a higher good.

3: Expression

The 3 points to an emotionally needy and sensitive soul (whether or not outwardly visible to others) — a romantic whose acute sensitivity makes criticism especially painful but also helps them intuitively tune in to and connect with others. The 3 centers around a powerful drive for self-expression — through speaking, writing, music, art, public relations, coaching, or teaching. If the expressive drive of those with 3 is blocked, stifled, or obstructed, they can get moody, depressed, or manipulative (hinting at rather than clearly expressing what they need). In the negative, 3 energy takes the form of complaining, sarcasm, insults, gossip, or cutting wit; in the positive, those with 3 in their birth number bring creative, constructive, encouraging, uplifting, enthusiastic expression. The biggest 3 hurdle is an innate feeling of self-doubt (a sense of being unprepared or not capable enough). The courage to push past this hurdle enables those with 3 to bring uplifting expression into the world.

4: Stability

The 4 represents a deep call to structure and stability, but with tendencies to do the opposite. Those with 4 in their birth number are ambitious and gregarious problem solvers with a natural analytical ability; thus, they make excellent managers and organizers. But 4 indicates a tendency to overanalyze that can lead to a sense of confusion, so writing down options and listening to gut feelings can help. Those with 4 have innate strength that can turn to stubbornness, because they view themselves, others, and the world as they "should" be. Like those with 2, those with 4 are so responsible they need to resign as "general managers of the universe." Those with 4 benefit immensely from using a clear, step-by-step process to accomplish their goals. Practicing anything over time, or engaging in a construction project, can be immensely helpful. When they balance strength with flexibility, and analysis with intuition, and temper impulsiveness with patience and persistence, they establish stable foundations in their lives and relationships, and can accomplish great things.

5: Freedom

The 5 represents freedom — a drive to experience many facets of life. Those working 5 are vivacious, quick-minded, multifaceted individuals who can see life from many angles, but their wide variety of interests can leave them scattered or burned out. Easily bored, they seek drama and excitement — or they create it. Most of these freedom-loving people favor new experience or adventure (direct or vicarious) over security or money in the bank. They have a powerful a drive to rescue others and to fight for the underdog. A notable challenge for those with 5 is a tendency to swing from dependence to independence — so they benefit from establishing interdependent relationships and healthy self-reliance in their own lives. Their key to freedom is discipline in the form of clear priorities and focus — digging one well one hundred feet deep rather than ten wells ten feet deep. Ultimately, in helping to liberate others, they find their own freedom.

6: Vision

The 6 points to high ideals and standards of beauty, purity, justice, fairness, and authenticity. But idealism can lead to disappointment, since few people or situations live up to the initial expectations of those working 6.

Disillusion is a big word for them, both in the negative sense of disappointment and in the positive sense of freedom from illusions — maturing into realism and a sense of perspective. In a group-learning environment, those with 6 tend to compare themselves to the most accomplished — and even if they do twenty things well, they tend to focus on a single mistake. Once they replace perfectionism with perspective, and learn to accept life as it is, they learn to celebrate their progress rather than obsess about so-called mistakes in the past. As those working 6 come to appreciate the innate perfection of life unfolding as it is, in its own good time, their strong sense of duty and commitment contributes to their vision of a better world.

7: Trust

The 7 centers around issues of trust — of self, others, and life unfolding. The 7 is an introspective, insightful energy, and those working it possess incisive minds that can read between the lines. Natural scholars and researchers (or hermits, despite a social persona), those with 7 favor and need solitude. Their private, suspicious, individualistic nature — and tendency to overshare or undershare what they're thinking or feeling — can lead to misunderstandings, which they may view as betrayals.

Those working 7 are here to learn to trust their own bodies, instincts, and sense of discernment rather than relying mostly on the guidance of books, experts, and the theories of others (including conspiracy theories). Otherwise clear and capable, they can refresh and re-vitalize their spirits out in the natural world, whether garden, beach, desert, or mountains. Once they learn to trust themselves, they finally establish trust with others through clear agreements — and achieve a relaxed openness in a world they can rely on.

8: Recognition

The 8 involves drives, struggles, mixed feelings, and deep satisfaction in the realm of material success — work, money, influence, self-control, and authority. Those with 8 may deny (even to themselves) an innate drive for recognition and may resent displays of wealth, power, or authority in others. Whatever their grades in school, those with 8 have powerful, logical, and strategic minds that see the path ahead and the writing on the wall, but (like those with 4) they need to follow a diligent process of effort over time to reach their goals. Because those with 8 like to make the rules rather than follow them, they sometimes need strong lessons to break through their resistance to feedback. Accepting their place in the material realm puts them in touch with their personal power to manifest their goals if only they step forward and follow through. They evolve and fulfill their calling through productive enterprise — sometimes philanthropic or humanitarian causes — achieving material success in service of a higher good.

9: Integrity

The 9 represents the one who leads the way — the wise man or woman whose life and example draw others to follow. However, this example of integrity and wisdom is achieved only after those working 9 overcome hurdles, learn the lessons of experience, and "get real." They may be slow to gain wisdom, but when they do so, they can be a great resource for others. Due to their depth and charisma, those working 9 find themselves in positions of leadership. They will either become role models of integrity or will suffer the consequences. They may have friends and family yet feel lonely due to a tendency to live in their own world of mental concepts and ideas at odds with reality. They have strong opinions and are also acutely sensitive to the opinions of others. Only when they free themselves from the "god of opinion" can they hear the god or goddess of their heart and find the wisdom that is their birthright and destiny, demonstrating the true value of leadership as they help light the way for others.

Putting It Together

This may be a good time to take a deep breath and let this information settle in. If you haven't read *The Life You Were Born to Live*, it may take a little while to absorb these highlighted issues and qualities associated with the primary "paths of potential" 1 through 9. Give yourself some time to explore how the descriptions may (or may not) apply to your past or present experience. All that follows is designed to further clarify the life-path information as it relates to the third purpose of life — your hidden calling and higher potential.

At this juncture it's entirely possible that you relate to issues in most or all of the nine categories: 1. We've all done something creative or felt insecure at times; 2. we've supported someone who took us for granted; 3. we've felt self-doubt or had trouble expressing ourselves; 4. we've felt impatient, stubborn, or confused or have acted impulsively; 5. we've desired independence or rooted for the underdog; 6. we've idealized someone who disappointed us or failed to meet our expectations; 7. we've needed alone time or felt betrayed;

8. we've wished to influence others or struggled with money; and 9. we've assumed a leadership role, had a slip of integrity, or needed a reality check.

I recognize many facets of the primary numbers in my own life as well, because all these issues are a part of the human experience. However, if each birth number were a suit of clothing, you might come to appreciate — after trying on different birth numbers (and related issues) — that your own birth number is indeed a better fit in expressing those strengths and challenges you have faced in the theater of your history and everyday life. For example:

- If you have 1 in your birth number, you will feel (or have felt) a need to prove yourself, and feel most on track when your creative juice is flowing.

- If you have 2 in your birth number, you will struggle (or have struggled) to balance giving with receiving, and feel most on track when your support is accepted and appreciated.

- If you have 3 in your birth number, you will feel (or have felt) self-doubt and emotional sensitivity, and feel most on track when you find a receptive listener.

- If you have 4 in your birth number, you will feel (or have felt) confused due to overanalysis, and feel most on track among family or other foundations in life.

- If you have 5 in your birth number, you will feel (or have felt) both dependent and independent, and feel most on track in the adventure of service to others.

- If you have 6 in your birth number, you will feel (or have felt) that you could have done better, and will feel most on track as you accept yourself and the world as it is.

- If you have 7 in your birth number, you feel (or have felt) betrayed, and will feel most on track as you learn to trust your body, your mind, and your life.

- If you have 8 in your birth number, you feel (or have felt) mixed emotions about money, fame, and authority, and will feel most on track as you gain recognition for excellent work in service of others.

- If you have 9 in your birth number, you feel (or have felt) clear messages about integrity, and feel most on track when leading and guiding by your example.

Individual Differences, Shared Patterns

No two individuals are exactly alike, even if they share the same life path. Even identical twins do not remain completely identical; they grow into unique personalities with their own interests. Factors including birth order, gender, family dynamics, and childhood experiences influence our choices and responses and help to shape our lives. No single tree on the planet is exactly like any other, yet we can accurately describe differences between redwoods and pines and birches.

Despite our individual differences, we humans also fall into recognizable patterns or life paths, each with common issues, potentials, and challenges. You'll work through those shared issues in your own way, in your own time. And your life may look radically different from the life of someone else on the same path if one of you is working through the issues in a more positive, constructive way, while the other animates the negative or destructive aspect.

Even though there are forty-five possible birth numbers shared among many millions of people born from 1900 to the present, you can speak of your birth number as a personal path — because you will experience and respond to those issues in your own unique way. There's ultimately no better or worse way to experience your life path. There's only living and learning.

You may recognize both negative and positive elements in your life as you reflect, with patience and compassion, upon your struggles and progress. Note where you've been, where you are at the present time, and where you're going — that is, who you're becoming. As you do so, bear in mind the often-repeated story of a conversation between an elder Native American and his grandson after the boy had gotten into some trouble: The grandfather says, "Within each of us live two wolves — one kind, productive, and peaceful; the other cruel, destructive, and hurtful."

"Which one is stronger inside me, Grandfather?" asks the boy.

"The one you feed," answers the elder.

This is the freedom and power within you: You can choose whether to animate the negative possibilities of your life path or to feed those more positive aspects as you mature and evolve through time in the school of life. This power of choice means it's never too late to follow your life path where it leads — never too late to fully live the life you were born to live.

Fundamentals on Your Life Path

To deepen and reinforce your understanding, here are some of the basic premises of the Life-Purpose System that relate to your life path.

First, your birth number(s) represent(s) the path you are here to ascend — it's an uphill climb — so what you are here to do isn't necessarily what comes easiest. In fact, your path brings special challenges as well as special potential. As you overcome the hurdles, you experience the benefits. This principle applies to every primary digit in anyone's birth number.

For example, those with 1 in their birth number — especially those with a double 1 (such as 19/10 or 29/11) — have higher creative potential but also feel the challenge of insecurity more acutely. So they won't always or immediately demonstrate creative flair or artistry; they may in fact show less creativity at first (or create in negative ways) until they overcome their insecurity and show the courage to be different, original, and to stand apart from the crowd.

An opposite example is also worth noting: My own birth number (26/8) does not contain the digit 1. This doesn't mean I necessarily lack creativity; rather, it means that I don't have the same sensitivities, challenges, or potential in this arena; that is, neither creativity nor insecurity is as central in my life as would be the case for people with 1 or double 1 in their birth number.

Second, as already noted, any life path has both negative and positive poles — and, more than any other factor, whether you work more in positive or negative ways will shape the course of your life. (The reasons one person chooses to create a software application and a second person comes up with a software virus could fill another book.)

Third, no life path is better (or worse) or easier (or more difficult) than any other; they are only different, each presenting distinct strengths and challenges.

Having understood these critical points about the life path numbers and how they work, you may want to review the nine life paths (or at least those related to primary digits in your birth number) in the context of what you now understand.

Consider the words of author Anya Seton: "There are many trails up the mountain, but in time they all reach the top." You were born with the drives, challenges, and gifts of your life path; what you do with them is up to you.

Life Paths, Career Paths

In their enthusiasm, those who have newly discovered the Life-Purpose System often hope that the information and insights they gain will help solve all the riddles in their lives, such as revealing the specific occupations or careers they should pursue, or predicting talent or success in a particular area.

For example, since those with an 8 as a predominant number have an innate drive to influence others, should they all become attorneys, politicians, or clerics? Should all those with a 1 (or double 1) go into creative arts of acting, music, or painting? Should those with a life path of 7, naturally inclined to solitude and scholarship, all become researchers? Should businesses groom all charismatic individuals with a 9 life path for leadership positions? Should those with a life path of 5, drawn toward saving others, go into search-and-rescue or social work?

The answer is no, because we are more (complicated) than our birth numbers. As much as I might like to present the Life-Purpose System as a solution to all career searches, your birth number is not intended to determine what kind of work you do in the world, but rather illuminates *how* you approach whatever work you do and the qualities you may bring to it.

Each individual, and each life path, brings different talents, qualities, and challenges to a given type of work. For example, in the field of acting, Meryl Streep, with a birth number of 33/6, demonstrates not only extraordinary sensitivity and expressive ability as a master of dialect (the double 3) but the high standards (of the 6) that impelled her to learn to play the violin in order to prepare for a role as a music teacher. The charismatic Robert Downey Jr. (29/11), with both the 9 and double 1, has abundant creative energy that enables him to do each take of a scene with inspiring originality, and is also a charismatic performer (reflecting the 9).

Streep and Downey each do great work but in qualitatively different ways reflecting their respective life paths. We find other respected actors (and people in every field) bringing their own unique approaches to their work — approaches that reflect not only the issues of their life paths but the genetic factors, life experience, timing, luck, and effort over time that all contribute to success in any given field. So no single path, and no particular number, is predictive of success or failure. We each bring our own unique combination of resources to our chosen career, calling, or craft as we climb a path to our potential.

Well-known individuals, in widely divergent fields, have throughout human history struggled in different ways with issues on their life paths — some working in the positive and others in the negative. For example: actor Paul Newman, singer-actress Barbra Streisand, astronaut Neil Armstrong, humanitarian César Chávez, inventor Alexander Graham Bell, comedian Groucho Marx, polio vaccine creator Dr. Jonas Salk, Olympian Jesse Owens, artist Michelangelo, and several popes all share the 26/8 life path — and so does Osama bin

Laden. And inspiring role model Helen Keller, visionary poet William Blake, humanitarian Coretta Scott King, Facebook founder Mark Zuckerberg, medical pioneer Dr. Karl Menninger, U.S. president Theodore Roosevelt, and philosopher Bertrand Russell all share the 32/5 life path — and so does Adolf Hitler. This sampling of quite different individuals known in a variety of fields all share similar strengths and challenges. How did they have such different impacts on the world? Most of these people overcame their challenges and applied their energy in positive, constructive, creative ways — while a few applied theirs in negative and destructive ways.

Never make the mistake of thinking that your birth number defines you as a person or limits your choices in the world. This system is intended to enhance, clarify, and focus insight and compassion (for self or others) — as a means of greater self-knowledge. The numbers only point toward resources you can bring to your chosen career and calling, as well as the hurdles you may encounter along the way.

Insight Isn't Enough

Conventional wisdom in some schools of psychotherapy and psychoanalysis posits that a breakthrough insight about our tendencies, past behavior, and formative or traumatic experiences will result in a catharsis and free us — opening the way to a new way of being, living, and doing. There's certainly value in healthy introspection and self-observation, as well as in a realistic assessment of our past and current tendencies, since awareness of a problem opens the way to finding a solution.

However, even after we gain insight into a problem, change can be slow and difficult — two steps forward, one step back. Knowing that we have a fear of elevators or of enclosed spaces, the dark, or insects — or even discovering a key incident when it all began — doesn't necessarily enable us to ride up to the sixtieth floor or relax in a small, dark closet with someone's pet tarantula.

I have a couple of friends who have undergone extensive therapy and who spend half their day analyzing their tendencies and the other half of the day dramatizing them. When they say things like, "Oh, I'm chronically late," or, "Whenever she acts that way I just blow my top," I want to respond, "Now that you know this, *what are you going to do about it?*"

Insight isn't enough. At best it provides a map, but we still have to make the journey. As I said earlier, just *thinking* about doing something is the same as not doing it. We know we've learned a lesson in the school of life only when our *actions* change.

When we explored the first purpose (learning life's

lessons), I introduced the school rules — the laws of reality. Certain laws have greater relevance than others, exerting specific leverage to help you overcome the hurdles on your life path — enabling you to *do* something, to take action, to change your behavior. Anyone interested in learning more about the laws most relevant to each life path will find them in the source book for the third purpose, *The Life You Were Born to Live*; they're also presented for more general application in *The Laws of Spirit*.

Keeping the Faith: Your Promise and Potential

Use the Life-Purpose System, combined with honest soul-searching and self-observation, to better understand yourself and your hidden calling — what you are truly here to confront and fulfill on the path to your full potential. What you do with that potential will reveal itself in the unfolding of your life and the fullness of time.

The extent to which you fulfill your hidden calling depends on how you respond to the challenges you meet along the way. No matter where you live, and whether you are born into poverty or privilege, you still have the responsibility, opportunity, and capacity to reach toward the highest light within you. But take to heart the higher truth that your life is unfolding as it should. We cannot predict, or force, where our path may lead — but we can bring a measure of grace to the journey with each small step we take.

Know that your path will guide you — you cannot lose your way. Because wherever you step, the path will appear beneath your feet. The way may twist and turn, and obstacles will appear as you continue onward and upward. But as my old mentor reminded me more than once, and I again remind you, "The way creates the warrior" — the climb itself develops the capacity to complete the journey. And the higher you climb, the better the view.

IF KNOWLEDGE IS POWER, you now wield the force of a deeper understanding of the first three purposes of life: learning essential lessons in the school of life; wisely choosing a satisfying career; and understanding your hidden or higher calling as you climb toward the peaks of your potential.

The Fourth Purpose

ATTENDING TO
THIS ARISING MOMENT

• *Pay Close Attention* • *Make Each Moment Count*

*There is surely nothing other
than the single purpose of the present moment.
A person's life is a succession of moment after moment.
When one fully understands the present moment,
there will be nothing else to do
and nothing else to pursue.*

— YAMAMOTO TSUNETOMO,
HAGAKURE (THE BOOK OF THE SAMURAI)

Consider for a moment the amount of territory you've covered in exploring the first three purposes of life: first, learning life's lessons, the school rules, and our human curriculum; second, applying tools for greater self-knowledge to help you choose a fulfilling career and calling; third, using an unusual method for determining, and focusing on, your life path (or deeper calling).

All this information can feel overwhelming. How can you organize it, distill it, and apply it in everyday life? To that end, it's time to bring it all home with the last piece of the puzzle — the fourth purpose, which integrates the first three purposes and brings them all into the simplicity and power of this present moment.

No matter what life brings — joys and disappointments, burdens and delights — amid all the complications, duties, and responsibilities, you can always handle this arising moment. *Now* is where you gain entry to the fourth purpose of life.

The Man Who Had No Purpose

Over the years, in addition to writing, speaking, and teaching, I've also offered one-on-one coaching — sometimes by phone and sometimes in person at my home in Northern California. One day a man I'll call Peter came to my home for a session. We greeted each other, he paid the agreed-upon fee in advance, and then I began with a key question: "What's your purpose for coming here? What would you like to accomplish?"

When I asked Peter this question, he just sat there, looking down at the floor, before he answered, "I don't know — I have no purpose."

"Well, if you did know your purpose, what might it be?"

Peter shook his head and repeated, "I have no purpose. None at all."

I thought about this, then explained, "This session is based entirely on what you want to accomplish, Peter, and since you're certain you have no purpose, I can only thank you for coming by. Nice meeting you. Now could you close the door on your way out?"

Surprised and a little disoriented, Peter stood up and

started moving toward the door, but then he turned and said, "Wait a minute! I traveled quite a distance to get here, and I just paid you some good money for ninety minutes of your time!"

Smiling, I said, "You know what? I think you've discovered a purpose. Please sit down."

This bit of Zen trickery on my part helped Peter to see that he did indeed have a purpose — to spend ninety minutes with me. And when our session was over, I promised Peter, he would discover another purpose — finding his way back to his car, opening the door, getting in, putting on his seat belt, starting the car, and driving to wherever he was going (without hitting any people or objects on the way). And then, when he arrived at his destination, another purpose would appear.

I then told Peter a brief conversation that took place at the funeral of a great Hasidic master. When a visitor, paying her respects, asked a longtime disciple, "What was the most important thing to your teacher?" he responded, "Whatever he happened to be doing at the moment."

I reminded Peter that the purpose of today is today. The same is true of each moment.

Peter had convinced himself that he had no purpose because he hadn't yet grasped a larger mission for his life. But he had failed to notice what may be the most important purpose of all — the one that appears before each of us, moment to moment. Such moments are the building blocks that form the foundation on which we build our lives.

Attention to this arising moment has been advocated by many different sages, at different times, in a variety of cultures. Yale professor William Phelps said, "I strive to live each day as if it were the first one I had ever experienced, and the last one I would ever live." Zen sword master Taisen Deshimaru reminded his students, "Be happy here and now or you never will be." And writer Barbara Rasp points out, "It's only possible to live happily ever after on a moment-by-moment basis."

We learn life's lessons (the first purpose), we choose our career and calling (the second purpose), and we fulfill our life path and hidden calling (the third purpose) all *in this present moment*. Welcome to the fourth purpose of life. You have arrived. No matter where you go, and no matter what the clock-face reads, you are always right here, right now.

What Snood Taught Me about Life

Snood is not an Eastern guru or relative of my mentor Socrates. Snood is not even a person, but rather an online game, and an addictive one at that. Like most addictive games, it seduces through simplicity: You shoot a little, round colored bubble, aiming to hit groups of same-colored bubbles; if your aim is true, they vanish, and the goal is to make as many bubbles as possible disappear. Other than developing a measure of aim (so presumably you can dissolve other colored bubbles you may encounter in the real world), Snood provides a few moments (or many nonproductive hours) of immersion and diversion; it's fair to consider it a shadow form of meditation, a sport without exercise, an insular activity.

But there's one beautiful, largely hidden facet of Snood that may reveal a transcendental teaching about life — and about living in the moment freshly, innocently, and without judgment or expectation. Does this wondrous revelation I'm about to share justify the hours I spend manipulating my mouse in hopes of topping my last score? Probably not. Or maybe so, depending on what you do with what I am about to share. Perhaps my wasted hours were not so wasted after all.

So here it is, my revelation: Every five shots or so, the entire configuration of all those bubbles shifts. What was, is no longer the same. It all changes, just like life. Any plan or strategy I might have formed for the next shot is now useless. Any regrets or resistance is pointless — again, same as in daily life. It's a whole new ball (or bubble) game. You have to shift your mental course instantly, look again, freshly, and address what is here and *now*, in this arising moment.

Everything changes — again and again. Each time the demand is the same: What now? What's my purpose in this moment? Snood taught me to linger not on what almost was, what could have been, or what might have or should have been but rather on what is, right now. As Marcus Aurelius wrote, "Time is a river of passing events. No sooner does one thing appear in sight than it is washed away, and another appears in its place. And this, too, shall be washed away." Each moment unfolds like waves breaking on the shore. If you're knocked down by one wave, rise again and ready yourself for the next one. Wave by wave, moment by moment.

Life as a Series of Moments

The entirety of our lives consists of a series of moments; as poet Emily Dickinson wrote, "Forever is composed of moments." No one is intelligent or kind or cruel or neurotic or saintly or enlightened or funny or sad all the time. But some of us have more intelligent, kind, cruel, neurotic, saintly, enlightened, funny, or sad moments. One realistic aim might be to increase the number of kind, enlightened, intelligent, or happy moments.

While we live, we're doing something in every moment. That doing may be sleeping and dreaming, or laughing or playing, or sitting very still in meditation, or writing or stretching. Life consists of action (or stillness) moment to moment. So even if you tend to dream big, start small; then connect the dots. Those dots are made of moments.

What are you doing in this moment? Are you sitting on a chair or a sofa, treadmill or stationary bike? Maybe you're lying in bed, sitting at the table or under an umbrella at a resort or on a beach. Whatever your location, reading is likely your current purpose. Maybe you'll stop for a few moments, look up and around, take a breath, sip a drink, or bite into a snack — which then becomes your purpose in the moments that follow.

Each moment is a gift. And as the proverb goes, "One moment can change a day, one day can change a life, one life can change the world."

There's No Such Thing as a Future Decision

All decisions are made in the moment, for the moment. Trying to make a permanent decision is like trying to eat once and for all. Waves keep rolling in; circumstances change. Each new moment is fresh. Want to know what you've decided? Observe what you do.

Begin your training in making decisions (and living in the moment) by noting the following guidelines and observations.

All you have to decide is what you will do right now. That is the only decision you can make or will ever make. Decisions only matter in the moment: Resolutions are at best good intentions, so make them if you wish — then face the next moment, ride the next wave. What will you do now?

You only need to make a decision in the moment you need to make it. Deciding which college you're going to attend, which job you'll take, or which man or woman you'll date or marry isn't necessary until it's fish-or-cut-bait time. Meantime, don't agonize over it. Just do what you're naturally doing in the moment.

We only need to manage (or change) our lives in relevant moments. One of the primary sayings in Alcoholics Anonymous is "Take it one day at a time." In reality, all we have to do is take it one *moment* at a time. Those who experience a powerful compulsion to drink do not feel compelled all the time. There's no need for them to decide not to take a drink except when the impulse to do so arises. In that moment, they can decide not to drink and instead call a sponsor or attend a meeting.

Decisions get clearer the closer you are to having to make them. Making a decision about what you will do next year, or what you'll do when you retire, is extraordinarily difficult and usually ends up being inaccurate — guesswork at best. Again, it's only a wish or intention. Deciding what to do in this moment arises naturally from circumstances at hand.

This moment is all you need to handle. This is your moment of power.

We Cannot Grasp the Now

Any physicist will remind you that what we normally think of as "the present moment" doesn't have any objective reality — it doesn't actually exist. If you say the word *now* as quickly as possible, between the instant you begin to sound out "n—" and the time you reach "—ow," millions of nanoseconds have passed. As scientist and philosopher William James put it, "Where is it, this present moment? It has slipped from our grasp, fled ere we could touch it, vanished in the instant of becoming." This is the fleeting quality of the present moment.

Yet, paradoxically, all we have is the eternal present — we float downstream in the river of time, flowing with the current, thus remaining in perfect stillness. Just so, we move through time yet remain within the stillness of this moment. Past and future are both happening now. There is only now. *Wherever we go is now.*

Past is memory; future is imagination. Nice places to visit, but you don't want to live there. Purposes tied to past or future have no reality; they are phantom concepts conjured by the mind. Handle just what is in front of you. By attending to the fourth purpose — this arising moment — you find the simple life. Reality is where you are now — moving in stillness, floating with the current in the river of time, resting in the eternal present.

Refrain from comparing this moment with memories of the past or an imagined future, and you find contentment — here and now. As a Zen sage said, "When I'm hungry, I eat; when I'm thirsty, I drink; when I'm tired, I rest."

The Challenge of Attending to the Present

The challenge of attending to this arising moment can be demonstrated with a single question: How often do you consciously eat a meal? Consider this question carefully. When was the last time you only ate — not ate while reading or watching television or listening to the radio or talking or checking your phone or computer, but the last time you sat and ate, only ate — seeing the food, smelling, tasting, and savoring it, aware you were chewing and swallowing? When was the last time that eating was enough to engage your full attention? (This task is probably no easier for me than it may be for you.)

Much of the time, we humans are bored with the present. So the prime difficulty of learning to live in and attend to the present moment is that *we don't really want to*. It doesn't seem enough for us, because we're not really paying attention. Isn't it fascinating that we can immerse ourselves in a video game or movie for minutes or hours, yet we can hardly pay full attention to dinner for more than a few seconds? Our restless minds flit about from past to future, remembering, judging, regretting, replaying, anticipating, planning, expecting. And none of that has anything to do with this moment. As author Alan Watts wrote, "The power of memories and expectations is such that for most human beings the past and the future are...*more* real than the present."

One night in the gymnasium, after Socrates watched me fly from the high bar, perform a difficult aerial maneuver, and stick my landing, I raised my fists in elation and declared my workout over. I pulled off my sweatshirt and stuffed it into my workout bag, and we left the gym. As we headed down the hallway, he said, "You know, Dan, that last move you did was pretty sloppy."

"What are you talking about?" I asked. "That was the best dismount I've done in a long time."

"I'm not talking about the dismount," he responded.

"I'm talking about the way you took off your sweatshirt and stuffed it into your bag."

I realized I had treated one moment, doing gymnastics, as special — and another moment as ordinary. Socrates reminded me, once again, that there are no ordinary moments. This realization, this challenge, lies at the very crux of your life and will determine the quality of your every moment: Can you, will you, learn to love the present moment? Can you develop the capacity to show each arising moment the same attention that you might give to a cherished friend or a lover — or at least to an online game? Will you wake up to the inestimable value of each passing moment as it slips, like a grain of sand, through the hourglass of your remaining time here? To the extent that you pay attention to the moment, you will have fulfilled the promise of the fourth purpose of life.

The Gift of Life: A Matter of Perspective

You appeared from nowhere, born onto the material realm on this blue-green speck suspended, spinning, in a vast galaxy in the cosmos. You may ruminate on how or why you came to be, or contemplate where space ends, but you find no answers, because all great questions lead to wonder and awe — and perhaps a measure of gratitude for the miracle of being invited to the feast. In counting your blessings, you may experience a desire to give something back — thus begins the path of service, the fruit of your journey, the doorway to joy.

Imagine for a moment that, through a strange twist of fate, you wake up one morning and find yourself imprisoned — scheduled for execution at midnight. You gaze out through prison bars and see the first rays of your last sunrise. A rooster crowing in the distance sounds poignantly sweet. You feel greedy for every sight, sound, taste, and aroma that day, which passes so quickly! You eat your last meal as the shadows grow long outside. And as the sun sets, you say your final farewell to the light of day, for you will never again see the sun rise. Each passing minute draws you closer to your final good-bye, your last prayer, your last breath.

Such a final day awaits every one of us. We may know in advance that our end is near, or we may have only a few seconds' notice, or none at all. But when the executioner raises the ax, how many of us might want to cry out, "Please, another moment! Let me take one more sweet breath! Give me one more sight, one more sound, one more touch of my loved ones!"

Now would be a perfect time to look up and around, to listen, to breathe deeply, to spend some time in nature — whether mountain, beach, or garden — to touch your loved ones, and to bring your best to life while you have the life to spend. How much time, how many more moments, that may be, no one can say.

Life itself is a near-death experience — ephemeral and brief. One among billions, you go on, loving, serving, grieving, and celebrating, seeking meaning and fulfillment. Now you understand that every life represents a hero's journey, and every moment counts.

The Highest Practice of All

We *do* things all the time — we do the dishes, do the laundry, do the shopping. We go to work and dig or type or lift or speak. But few of us *practice*. The key difference between doing and practicing is this: When you practice an action, you aren't merely repeating by rote but rather are striving to improve or to refine whatever you are doing — whether it's signing your name, opening a door, carrying groceries, merging with traffic, or folding laundry.

We're familiar with practicing a sport or a dance or a game or a musical instrument. Naturally, in these formal training activities, we understand that we want to improve our stroke or leap or swing or strum. We treat these activities as somehow special and separate from the practice of everyday life, as if they were more deserving of our full attention. Which is why Socrates once said to me, "The difference between us, Dan, is that you practice gymnastics; I practice everything."

Think of it! What would it be like to practice every moment and everything we do? To attend to how we lift a forkful of food to our mouths, and breathe, and chew — to attend to the words we speak and how we speak them. I grant you, in the hands of some of our more obsessive or neurotic friends, this idea of practicing everything might take the shape of a compulsive, never-ending self-improvement program. But that isn't at all the point.

The practice I'm recommending creates an art of living. Your life becomes an art form. Your performance is unique — unlike any other — because no one else can live your life as you can. When you *practice* all that you do, your attention naturally returns to each arising moment. You step into the flow. You enter the zone. You become a cloud drifting through the skies, neither racing ahead of the wind nor dragging behind, but moving naturally, once again in harmony with what the Chinese sages called the Tao.

This is my practice. I remain something of a beginner, but a devoted one. I practice with the faith in this principle — that we improve over time. The first step is to form the sincere intention to respect each passing moment and treat each action as you would a performance before thousands. How you do anything is how you do everything, which is why the Zen masters say, "If you can serve tea properly, you can do anything." In mastering anything, you master yourself. So ask yourself, in random moments: Am I breathing? Am I relaxed? Am I moving with grace?

The concept of a Way is a foundation stone of the Eastern spiritual traditions, which gave us the arts of flower arranging, calligraphy, the tea ceremony, and many of the martial disciplines, as well as the art of sitting or walking meditation — not as ends in themselves, but to light the way, to refresh our hearts and minds, to provide a template in the art of living and a doorway to the kind of ego dissolution in moments of absorption that we enjoyed as young children. What we have lost, we can find again. This is how we "become like little children" to enter the "kingdom of heaven."

Practice whatever you do. Notice the small things — the subtle shift of posture that relieves stress, the relaxing breath, the act of remembering to smile for the pleasure of it. Six words: Here and now, breathe and relax. Practice that in all you do, and your life will change for the better.

Despite what you may have heard about "just being" — or the notion that "it's not about what you do but about who you are" — I beg to differ. I propose that in terms of our influence on and existence in the world around us, you are (largely) what you do. So changing your behavior changes your identity, moment to moment.

You don't have to think positive thoughts. You don't have to feel peaceful or confident or compassionate or happy or loving — you only need to behave that way, as much as you can, whenever you remember to do so. This practice animates and celebrates the best of your humanity and spirit. This practice reflects the heart of the *peaceful warrior's way.*

The fourth purpose of life, which integrates and distills the other three purposes into one manageable moment at a time, is a lifelong practice. Calling forth all you have learned on your journey, you can transform everyday life into a path of personal evolution and infuse each moment with new meaning and purpose.

Attend to this moment with each breath. And in random moments, silently ask yourself, "What is my purpose in this arising moment?" Then do whatever needs to be done, in a wondrous and changing parade of purposes that shape the story of your life, and of all our lives.

Epilogue

OUR SPIRITUAL PURPOSE

If Earth is a school, then what does graduation feel like? What's waiting for you on the mountaintop? Could your life be more mysterious than you can see from the valley of conventional awareness? Since ancient times, mystics and shamans have consulted with oracles and sought to communicate with the spirit world, while countless others have simply gazed up into the night sky or looked deep within to find answers. It seems fitting here to complete our exploration of the four purposes of life by addressing the larger spiritual purpose of our existence.

I relate the story of my own spiritual journey in *Way of the Peaceful Warrior*. Many readers have told me that the book changed their lives. Few are able to articulate exactly what changed, but I believe it comes down to this: The story describes my shift from a narrow focus on personal success to an understanding of life's bigger picture — and readers share that experience.

In the film adaptation of my first book, the full scope of the quest gives way to a smaller story about a young gymnast who learns nuggets of wisdom, culminating in a deeper understanding of the power of the present moment. In other words, the film ends with the fourth purpose of life.

But this epilogue, like my first book, takes us beyond self-improvement to what may be humanity's ultimate purpose — transcendence, usually defined as rising above or beyond. Any dictionary definitions fall short, because the experience, by its very nature, goes beyond conventional language and defies description, which is why Lao-tzu said, "Those who know do not speak [of it], and those who speak [of it] do not know."

Many of the sages and saints who have seen the light, or truth or reality as it is, have felt moved to provide clues, methods, metaphors, and paths pointing toward that which defies description. For example, Zen masters assign their students *koans* — riddles that can't be solved by the rational mind (such as "What was your original face before you were born?"). The *koan* stretches the student's awareness to leap beyond conventional mind to experience *kensho*, a breakthrough insight similar to, yet transcending, the "aha" experience of solving a more conventional riddle.

Zen *koans* are but one way to facilitate an awakening. Seeking to achieve a state of liberation or bliss, Sufi masters twirl and dance, while other seekers go on vision quests or ingest psychotropic substances; still others pray, contemplate, meditate, chant, or do practices involving breath and visualization. All for a glimpse of the transcendent.

Why do they bother? Isn't this conventional world, and everyday life, enough? Perhaps transcendence doesn't really exist except in the minds of true believers. Maybe ideas about the divine, and soul and spirit, and heavenly realms during or after physical death, are fanciful notions or flights of imagination. Our souls may or may not ascend to a heavenly realm, and even if we have past or future lives, we're not likely to remember any of them with certainty, but we certainly do have to live *this* life.

Yet, in moments of awe and wonder — or more often when tragedy strikes, in times of great dislocation, distress, or when dealing with mortality — we are moved to ask the existential questions, such as "Why live if we must die?" and "What is my purpose here?" At times like these, the possibility of a divine intelligence, a prime mover or creative source and substance of the universe, can seem not only appealing but somehow self-evident. (As one religious scholar put it, "There's God, then there's not paying attention.") After all, innumerable sages, mystics, and clerics in holy orders, who have devoted their lives to the quest for Spirit, God, or Truth, report how the "gates of heaven" appeared as they broke through the illusions of conventional mind to glimpse the truth that sets us free — a vision of the eternal and absolute Consciousness at the heart of our existence. They call us to turn our eyes upward toward our spiritual purpose even as we live our day-to-day lives; to merge heaven and earth with a leap of faith; to live with our heads in the clouds and our feet on the ground.

Most of the time conventional reality monopolizes our attention. We have daily tasks, duties, pleasures, and problems. We play out our dramas in the theater of gain and loss, desire and satisfaction. We pursue fulfillment, pleasure, and success, trying to make life work out according to our hopes and wishes. No matter what our degree of success or status, we experience attachment, anxiety, and disappointment in this world of change. This realization can set in motion a sincere and open-minded quest to realize a higher or transcendent truth.

One way to understand the difference between conventional and transcendental awareness is to imagine the experience of lying on your belly down in a valley and examining stones, weeds, and grass versus standing on a mountain peak and surveying the panorama below. Both experiences have value, but only one provides the bigger picture. To enjoy the panorama, we need to make the climb. But in daily life, this shift of awareness can take place in an instant. When we make this shift — remembering life's bigger picture even as we function in everyday life — the conventional and transcendental worlds become one.

Seeking the transcendent does not mean rejecting our conventional world but rather embracing it fully, releasing our resistance, attachments, and expectations. As we do, we experience a lighthearted wisdom; we take ourselves and our dramas less seriously. A momentary glimpse of the transcendent can restore our humor and refresh our spirits, which is why many awakening individuals consider our spiritual purpose the ultimate quest even as we do the laundry, care for children, and work for a better world.

Freedom and joy do not reside elsewhere; they are right here, right now, right before our eyes. All paths, and the four purposes I've shared in this book, lead toward an awakening where theories and concepts, models and maps all dissolve into the eternal present, into reality as it is.

The four purposes not only lend meaning to our lives but also provide the foundation for this great spiritual purpose: the quest for illumination. Once we come full circle and complete this "journey without distance," we recognize that we've been here before. We have always been right here, precisely where we stand, in this arising moment of absolute mystery and divine perfection.

In quiet moments, many of us are touched by the wonder, miracle, and mystery at the heart of our existence. As expressed in the epigraph below, from my novel *The Journeys of Socrates*, my old mentor, after an arduous odyssey, comes to the following conclusion, which speaks to a realization awaiting us all.

> *When I was young, I believed that life*
> *might unfold in an orderly way,*
> *according to my hopes and expectations.*
> *But now I understand that the Way winds like a river,*
> *always changing, ever onward, following God's gravity*
> *toward the Great Sea of Being.*
> *My journeys revealed that the Way itself creates the warrior;*
> *that in the fullness of time,*
> *every path leads to peace, and every choice to wisdom.*
> *And that life has always been, and will always be,*
> *arising in Mystery.*

— DAN MILLMAN, *THE JOURNEYS OF SOCRATES*

Acknowledgments

Each book has its own story to tell, and its own cast of characters. Most, like this one, begin as a solitary enterprise — an idea in the author's mind, an impulse that becomes a mission. Then the lonely hours of isolation, confronting and filling empty page after page in the first creative outpouring. But sooner or later, the author needs others to provide feedback, perspective, and editorial guidance.

Many helped in this process: My wife, Joy, my daughter Sierra, and my friend Doug Childers volunteered to hack and hew their way through the thicket of verbiage that made up the first rough draft, looking for paragraphs worth rescuing, helping me clear away the overgrowth so that the second draft resembled something more like a landscaped garden, with ideas deserving further cultivation laid out in orderly rows.

I was then ready to show the manuscript to publisher Linda Kramer of H J Kramer Inc., which publishes in collaboration with New World Library. She immediately saw its potential and made an offer on the spot. I now had a committed publishing house for this work in progress.

Then a group of readers, including Martin Adams, Holly Deme, Alex Deme, Peter Ingraham, David Moyer, and Beth Wilson, helped further refine the material.

Through additional rewriting, I sent the manuscript to freelance editor Nancy Carleton, who operated with surgical precision on a line-by-line edit, inspiring additional writing before I handed the completed manuscript to the editorial and production team at New World Library. There the manuscript received further refinement by editors Kristen Cashman and Jason Gardner, then cover design by Alan Hebel and Ian Shimkoviak of the Book Designers, typesetting by Tona Pearce Myers, and proofreading by Karen Stough, as well as marketing and publicity planning by Munro Magruder and Monique Muhlenkamp.

That's when Suezen Stone, H J Kramer's hardworking director of foreign rights, contacted publishers overseas to invite offers on the new book.

It takes a village not just to raise a child but also to help bring a book to full fruition and send it out into the world. I'm grateful to each and all.

Further Resources

SOURCE MATERIAL

If you would like to explore the following topics more deeply, I refer you to the source books, from which I've drawn material to present within the context of *The Four Purposes of Life*.

Required Courses and Curriculum on Planet Earth

No Ordinary Moments: A Peaceful Warrior's Guide to Daily Life
Dan Millman (H J Kramer/New World Library)

As indicated by the subtitle, this book presents fundamental practices of the peaceful warrior's way and the school of daily life, and contains sections dealing with issues such as universal addictions and energy management not found in my other books.

Everyday Enlightenment: The Twelve Gateways to Personal Growth
Dan Millman (Grand Central Publishing)

The course catalog and curriculum presents a summary introduction of each subject in the school of life. *Everyday Enlightenment* offers an in-depth treatment of these twelve arenas of life.

School Rules

The Laws of Spirit: A Tale of Transformation
Dan Millman (H J Kramer/New World Library)

This book relates an adventure in the mountains with a mysterious woman sage who reveals specific laws of spirit, including balance, choices, process, action, surrender, and unity, and describes how they apply in everyday life.

The Nine Life Paths

The Life You Were Born to Live: A Guide to Finding Your Life Purpose
Dan Millman (H J Kramer/New World Library)

The summary descriptions of each of the nine life-path numbers provide a brief introduction to a far more comprehensive treatment of the Life-Purpose System presented in this book. (Also see the Life-Purpose App at the iTunes store.)

Tales of Transcendence

Bridge Between Worlds: Extraordinary Experiences That Changed Lives
Dan Millman and Doug Childers (H J Kramer/New World Library)

This book speaks to readers who appreciate documented stories that stretch our imaginations and remind us of the mysterious nature of life — and those who enjoy dramatic reminders of life's intriguing possibilities.

Final Epigraph
(Permission to reprint courtesy of HarperOne Publishers)

The Journeys of Socrates: A Novel
Dan Millman (HarperOne Publishers)

This Russian odyssey, beginning with a death and birth in 1872, relates the life, the ordeals, and the evolution of the man I would years later name Socrates. It's a story about how a boy became a man, how a man became a warrior, and how a warrior found peace.

Appendix

DETERMINING YOUR LIFE-PATH NUMBER
BY DOING THE MATH

If you can add a few numbers together (such as 2 + 4 + 3 + 6), you can compute your birth number in three simple steps:

1. Write out an accurate date of birth numerically: For example: <u>April 20, 1975</u>, becomes 4-20-1975. *Note:* Be sure to include all four digits of the year, as in <u>1975</u> (not '75) or <u>2010</u> (not '10).

2. Add up every single digit to form a sum. In this example: $4 + 2 + 0 + 1 + 9 + 7 + 5 = \underline{28}$. *Note:* Be sure to separate all digits. So for April 20, you would add <u>4</u> + <u>2</u> + <u>0</u> (*not* 4 + 20).

3. Once you have a sum — in this example, <u>28</u> — you then "resolve" these two digits by adding them together to make a final sum, so 28 becomes

$\underline{2} + \underline{8} = \underline{10}$ — and the final *birth number* is written (in this example) as $\underline{28/10}$.

Other examples:

- October 20, 1988: 10-20-1988 — $1 + 0 + 2 + 0 + 1 + 9 + 8 + 8 = 29$, resolved to $\underline{29/11}$ (a four-digit birth number).

- March 3, 1960: 3-3-1960 — $3 + 3 + 1 + 9 + 6 + 0 = 22$, resolved to $\underline{22/4}$ (a three-digit birth number).

- February 20, 2003: 2-20-2003 — $2 + 2 + 0 + 2 + 0 + 0 + 3 = \underline{9}$ (a single-digit birth number).

Be sure to check your math; even though it is simple addition, you want to make sure your calculations are correct. (I encourage you to check your results via the life-purpose calculator at www.peacefulwarrior.com, which also provides additional information.)

Further Information

You can find more details on birth numbers and the Life-Purpose System, including answers to other common questions, in *The Life You Were Born to Live* (see Further Resources) or by downloading the Life-Purpose App (available for the iPhone and other mobile devices).

About the Author

Dan Millman — a former world champion gymnast, coach, martial arts instructor, and college professor — teaches an approach to living with greater clarity and compassion, in the present moment, with a peaceful heart and a warrior spirit. He is the author of the bestselling classic *Way of the Peaceful Warrior* (adapted to a feature film in 2006) and numerous other books read by millions of people in twenty-nine languages. Dan teaches worldwide, and over the past three decades has influenced men and women from all walks of life, including leaders in the fields of health, psychology, education, business, politics, sports, entertainment, and the arts.

For details: www.peacefulwarrior.com